FLOURISH

A

take up & READ

PUBLICATION

Editorial Director: Elizabeth Foss

Copy Editors: Carly Buckholz, Emily DeArdo and Rosie Hill

Illustration, Cover Art, & Calligraphy: Kristin Foss

Cover Photography: Colleen Connell

Research & Development: Elizabeth Foss, Emily DeArdo, and Colleen Connell

ISBN-13: 978-1727138276

ISBN-10: 1727138279

COMMUNITY

VISIT US

takeupandread.org

BE SOCIAL

Facebook @takeupandread

Instagram @takeupandread

Twitter @totakeupandread

SEND A NOTE

totakeupandread@gmail.com

CONNECT

#TakeUpAndRead

#FlourishStudy

Before he had traveled to Rome and met the growing Christian community there, St. Paul wrote the letter to the Romans. The letter is a preparation to aid these new Christians to flourish spiritually, both individually and as a community. He wrote to introduce himself to the Romans, and to outline for them how to live a life of grace in faith. At the time of this correspondence, Rome was the cultural center of the world; it boasted a vast network of roads and an effective system of communication. The city stood apart as both a reality and a symbol of the greatness of civilization. Because all roads lead to Rome, Christianity was flourishing there at the time of Paul's letter, but the relationship of Christians to the Roman authorities was fraught with tension. Christ's apostles steadfastly insisted that the early Christian community there respect the government and bear witness to the Lord, in part, by their exemplary citizenship.

At once a grand message of the mercy of God for the whole world— every tribe of Israel and believing Gentiles alike—and a treatise delineating practical instruction for living a holy Christian life, this epistle is the essential gospel of Jesus Christ. Because we are assured that it is the inspired Word of God, we know that the Holy Spirit intended it for us, too. It is the most precise distillation of the gospel message in the New Testament, and as we study it, we have a clear sense that God knew that we would also need exactly this letter for times such as these in which we live.

Paul's letter, which is thought to have been written by him in Corinth and delivered to Rome by Phoebe, a deaconess, focuses on preaching the salvation we have in Christ's life, death, and resurrection. Because there was some tension about who was worthy of salvation between Christian converts from Judaism and Christian converts from paganism, he affirmed wholeheartedly that no one is more worthy than anyone else of the redemption Christ earned for us on the cross. As a matter of fact, as sinners, we are all equally unworthy. Redemption is a gift offered to everyone freely and we are saved by the grace earned for us by Christ on the cross and the victory won in his resurrection. The only response to such a gift is to return love for love. As Christians, we act on the grace received out of love for the God who gave it, and our works become our faith alive in us.

St. Paul delves deep into the mysteries of sin, and he acknowledges the struggle against it. He reminds his Roman readers—and us—that sin has spread as if it were a plague, infecting pagans (Romans 1:18-32) and the people of Israel (Romans 2:1-30). It is Jesus who pours grace into the festering sin and justifies the sinner, healing by and for heaven.

To be a Christian in the early church and in the world today is to be both a citizen of the state and a member of the body of Christ. St. Paul calls upon the Romans to see themselves as the Church, to understand that they are members of the ecclesial body of Christ. His words to them give us clear direction even when the times in which we live might seem to lack holy ecclesial leadership. The Book of Romans empowers us to see that we are the Church, and then it tells us exactly how to be the Church.

As you prepare for each day's study, you'll notice that we've given you a large swath of reading (usually a chapter) and then highlighted a focus passage. Please turn to your Bibles and read the entire large passage before reading the devotional essay. Ask yourself what essential gospel point was Paul communicating to the Romans with those words. And then consider an experience or aspect of your personal faith journey where that same essence of the gospel was able to flourish, is currently flourishing, or where you hope will lead to a flourishing of your faith. We encourage you to employ the time-tested *Lectio Divina* method of study. Please see page 112 for a thorough explanation of how that can work in your time with Scripture. Remember to consider how personal spiritual growth contributes to the flourishing community of believers in which we live out our faith. Then, maybe jot the focus verse on a slip of paper and tuck it into a pocket to take with you as you carry out your mission in the world each day.

There is a clarion call today to rebuild Christ's Church, a plea for the laity to dig deep and rise with Christ to bring his light to a world wracked by sin. Let there be no confusion: by our baptism, each of us has been made priest, prophet, and king. This epistle from the good and holy St. Paul contains what we need to flourish in those roles, to be both prayerful and active. Let us give this essential gospel our full attention. Let it inspire us, embolden us, and empower us.

Let us flourish in the faith.

Elizabeth Foss
Founder, Take Up & Read

Let there be no confusion:
by our baptism, each of
us has been made priest,
prophet, and king. This
epistle from the good and
holy St. Paul contains
what we need to flourish
in those roles,
to be both prayerful
and active.

Intentional Design

Each of our studies is created with unique, intentional design. We want to connect you with the Word and keep you connected throughout the day. In this Scripture study, we begin by introducing context for St. Paul, the author of Romans. We walk through each chapter of Romans together, and provide a short focus verse with a devotional essay. We encourage *Lectio Divina* ("holy reading") for each chapter. For detailed guidance on *Lectio Divina*, please see page 112. As always, fresh layouts, font design, and original artwork ensure that you have the tools to keep him close to your heart, every day.

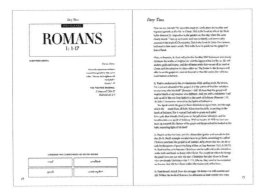

DAILY FOCUS READING

This Scripture study includes daily focus readings and essays. Notations for the full chapter and further reading are provided so you can open your Bible and further explore the Word.

LECTIO DIVINA

Reflect upon the Word and make a deep connection with your daily life by keeping the components of *Lectio Divina* in mind.

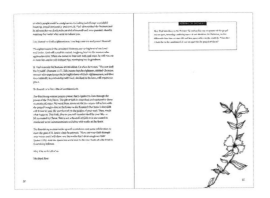

ACTIO

Following the daily essays are *Actio* prompts for you to reflect upon in your heart or to respond directly on the page.

NEW RECIPES

Each week, we encourage you to try a new recipe and share it with your community.

WEEKLY SCRIPTURE VERSE

We will memorize one key verse to reflect upon each week.

SELAH

Here is a chance to pause for prayer, praise, and rest.

At Take Up & Read, we want you to discover what prompts and pages are most useful to your spiritual journey of faith with Christ. There is no perfect way to perform *Lectio Divina*—the important thing is that you take the time to have a conversation with God, using Christ's Word as your guide.

Let us

flourish

in the faith.

Saul

BIRTH

- Born in Tarsus, a town in the Roman province of Cilicia, around 5 AD
- A Jew of the Tribe of Benjamin
- Also possessed Roman citizenship, which entitled him to some important legal rights

EARLY LIFE

- Educated in Jerusalem by the famous rabbi Gamaliel
- Became a zealous member of the Pharisees
- One of the most erudite and learned figures in the early church

PERSECUTION OF CHRISTIANS

- First encountered the Christian faith in Jerusalem
- "Inveterate enemy" of the Church
- Present at St. Stephen's martyrdom
- Still a young man when he assumed a leading role in the Christian persecutions

CONVERSION

- Set out from Damascus to arrest Christians
- On the way, stopped by a vision of the risen and glorified Christ
- Left blind by the light, taken to Damascus where he sat in darkness for three days
- Baptized by Ananias, who had received a vision to go to Saul and lay hands upon him to cure his blindness and also to baptize him

AFTER CONVERSION

- Left Damascus and withdrew into Arabia for prayer and meditation
- Returned to Damascus and began preaching the faith
- Made a secret escape from the city to avoid being seized by the king's governor

to Paul

EARLY MINISTRY

- Went to Jerusalem and spent more than two weeks with St. Peter
- The Holy Spirit said, "Set apart for me Barnabas and Saul for the work to which I have called them," around 46 AD, at Antioch in Syria (Acts 13:2)
- *About his name:* Acts 13:9 mentions that "Saul is also called Paul." Even today, many orthodox Jews reserve one name for family and synagogue (a Jewish name), and a different name for business in the secular world (a Gentile name). "Saul" was his Jewish name, but "Paul" was his Gentile name. Once his mission to the Gentiles begins, Acts calls him Paul.

EXECUTION + DEATH

- Imprisoned again in Rome; wrote the second letter to Timothy
- Martyred by decapitation and his grieving friends carried his corpse to subterranean labyrinths for burial
- St. Paul-Outside-the Walls Basilica was built on site where Paul is said to have been buried

I have fought the good fight,
I have finished the race, I have kept the faith.
From now on there is reserved for me the crown of
righteousness, which the Lord, the righteous judge,
will give me on that day, and not only to me but also to
all who have longed for his appearing.

2 TIMOTHY 4:7-8

Missions

FIRST MISSIONARY JOURNEY

- Went with Barnabas and Mark to Cyprus and Asia Minor
- Brought the gospel message to Antioch, Pisidia, and Iconium; and founded communities there
- Able to reach both Jews and Gentiles with his teaching
- Preaching caused local disturbances
- Stoned by a mob and left for dead
- Returned to Antioch around 49 AD

SECOND MISSIONARY JOURNEY

- Set out around 50 AD with Silas, for a journey that lasted about two years
- Traveled to Tarsus, then revisited churches of Asia Minor
- Timothy joined him at Lystra
- Possible that he converted the Galatians at this time
- Told in a vision to go to Macedonia
- Crossed the Hellespont waterway (now known as Dardanelles), and brought the faith to Europe
- In Philippi, converted his first convert, Lydia, a Macedonian
- Briefly imprisoned, then went to Thessalonica, Beroea, and Athens
- In Athens, encountered Greek philosophers, including Stoics and Epicureans, who listened to him, but were not persuaded
- Went to Corinth, where he stayed for over a year, establishing a solid Christian community there
- Left Greece and went to Palestine to rejoin the church in Antioch

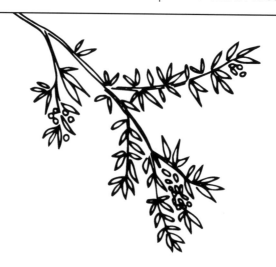

+ Imprisonment

THIRD MISSIONARY JOURNEY

- Around 53 A.D. traveled again to Asia Minor and then went to Ephesus, where he stayed for two years
- Wrote First Letter to the Corinthians while in Ephesus
- In Ephesus, the craftsmen who made statues of the god Artemis rioted when their businesses were affected by the change in religious practice, making it dangerous for Paul to stay
- Went to Philippi in Macedonia, where he wrote Second Corinthians
- Proceeding to Corinth, wrote LETTER TO THE ROMANS
- On his way back to Jerusalem, met the elders of the Church at Ephesus
- Premonition of his imprisonment and martyrdom

IMPRISONMENT + JOURNEY TO ROME

- Fifth visit to Jerusalem is last of which we have public record
- After glad reception by the brethren, was dragged out of the temple by a mob, attacked by Jewish enemies, and rescued by Roman soldiers
- Brought before Sanhedrin on charges of bringing Gentiles into the Temple (an offense against Jewish law and Roman law because the Roman law protected the Jews right to worship according to their laws)
- Managed to divide the council and, invoking his rights as a Roman citizen, was sent to Caesarea for trial before the governor
- Three charges were made before Felix, the Governor of Judea: inciting factious discord among all the Jews throughout the empire, heresy against the law of Moses as the leader of a sect of the Nazarenes, and profaning the temple at Jerusalem
- Jailed for two years
- Trial held under Festus, Felix's successor
- Paul appealed to Caesar and went to Rome; shipwrecked on island of Malta
- In Rome, put under house arrest for two years
- Probably wrote the "captivity epistles," Colossians, Philippians, Philemon, and Ephesians, while imprisoned in Rome

Day One

Memory

V E R S E

Week One

For I am not ashamed of the gospel; it is the power of God for salvation to everyone who has faith, to the Jew first and also to the Greek. For in it the righteousness of God is revealed through faith for faith; as it is written, "The one who is righteous will live by faith."

ROMANS 1:16-17

I will practice Scripture memory by:
- ○ Praying
- ○ Writing
- ○ Speaking
- ○ Reading
- ○ Other: _____

The One who is righteous will live by faith

ROMANS 1:17

OPEN YOUR BIBLE

ROMANS
1:1-17

SCRIPTURE NOTES:

Focus Verse

For in it the righteousness of God is
revealed through faith for faith; as it is
written, "The one who is righteous will
live by faith."
Romans 1:17

FOR FURTHER READING:
2 Samuel 7:10-17
Habakkuk 2:4

CONSIDER THE COMPONENTS OF LECTIO DIVINA

read	*meditate*
pray	*contemplate*

Day Two

Here we are, friends! We open this study to God's plans for healthy and vigorous growth in this life in Christ. Romans is the book to which the Holy Spirit directed St. Augustine in the garden on that fateful day when the saint clearly heard, "Take up and read." This is the book St. John Chrysostom had read to him once a week. This is the how-to guide for the gospel of Jesus Christ.

In Romans, St. Paul will echo the familiar Old Testament and clearly delineate the reality of original sin and the legacy it left for us. He will address guilt and shame, and the ultimate truth that we are all in need of Christ and the salvation he alone offers us. The Letter to the Romans will offer to us the gospel we need to flourish in this life and to live with our Lord forever in heaven.

St. Paul is exuberant in his proclamation of life-giving truth. He writes, "For I am not ashamed of the gospel; it is the power of God for salvation to everyone who has faith" (Romans 1:16). It's true that the gospel will require much of any woman who believes. And yet, with confidence, God calls us all to live our lives bathed in the spirit of holiness (Romans 1:4).

St. John Chrysostom writes that the Spirit of holiness is

> the Spirit which He gave to them that believe upon Him, and through which He made them all holy. Wherefore he saith, "according to the Spirit of holiness." For it was of God only to grant such gifts.

It is a gift, dear friends. God gives us the gift of our salvation, and he breathes into us a spirit of holiness. Will we receive it? Will we turn our faces up towards the shower of his grace and let ourselves be bathed in the holy, nurturing light of his love?

St. Paul is on fire for God, and it's a flame that ignites and spreads to this day. By St. Paul's example, we learn how to go forth, answering the call of Christ to proclaim the gospel to all nations, fully aware that we can do so only by the power of grace working within us (see Romans 12:3,6;15:15). St. Paul teaches us to become Christians and to walk within the discipline of the faith and hand-in-hand with Christ. The people to whom he brings the good news are not only the non-Christians, but also those in Rome who are already Christians (1:6-7, 15). Like us, they need to be reminded we live our best life for Christ within the framework of his laws.

St. Paul doesn't shrink from the struggle. He knows we will stumble and fall. Within the book of Romans, he delineates at least twenty-two ways in which people could be unrighteous, including such things as prideful boasting, sexual immorality, and envy. St. Paul admonished the Romans and he admonishes us: don't make an idol of yourself and your passions, thereby rejecting the Savior who came to redeem you.

Live instead in God's righteousness. Live hope and joy and peace! Flourish!

His righteousness is the abundant kindness and saving love of our Lord and Savior. God will reveal his sacred, forgiving heart to the woman who approaches him. When she comes to him with faith and trust, he will run out to meet her and he will embrace her, enveloping her in goodness.

St. Paul reminds the Romans of Habakkuk 2:4 when he writes, "The just shall live by faith" (Romans 1:17). This means that the righteous, faithful Christian woman who experiences the lovingkindness of God's righteousness, and then lives faithfully in relationship with God, obedient to his laws, will experience grace.

To flourish is to live a life of confident faith.

The flourishing woman prays a prayer that is ignited by love through the power of the Holy Spirit. The gift of faith is nourished and nurtured in those moments of prayer. We want those moments for you as you fall in love with the gospel brought alive in the Letter to the Romans! Our hope is that faith will flower in your life and flourish in the garden of your soul. Then, watch what happens. That faith alive in you will manifest itself by your life—a life animated by Christ. This is not a theoretical faith; it is one rooted in obedience to his commandments and alive with works of the Spirit.

The flourishing woman looks up with confidence and some exhilaration to meet the gaze of St. James when he entreats, "Show me your faith through your works and I will show you the works that I do through my faith" (James 2:18). And she opens her arms wide to the ripe fruits of a life lived in flourishing holiness.

May it be so for all of us.

Elizabeth Foss

Here Paul introduces to the Romans the notion that our acceptance of the gospel sets us apart, becoming a defining aspect of our identities. As Christians, we live differently from how we once did and how many others in the world do. What does it look like to live unashamed of and set apart for the gospel of Christ?

OPEN YOUR BIBLE

ROMANS

1:18-32

SCRIPTURE NOTES:

Focus Verse

For the wrath of God is revealed from heaven against all ungodliness and wickedness of those who by their wickedness suppress the truth. For what can be known about God is plain to them, because God has shown it to them. Ever since the creation of the world his eternal power and divine nature, invisible though they are, have been understood and seen through the things he has made. So they are without excuse; for though they knew God, they did not honor him as God or give thanks to him, but they became futile in their thinking, and their senseless minds were darkened. Claiming to be wise, they became fools; and they exchanged the glory of the immortal God for images resembling a mortal human being or birds or four-footed animals or reptiles.

Romans 1:18-23

FOR FURTHER READING:

Acts 17:30-31

CONSIDER THE COMPONENTS OF LECTIO DIVINA

read	*meditate*
pray	*contemplate*

Day Three

A couple months ago, my daughter performed in her final choral concert of the year. As we sat watching, my two-year-old squirmed, eager to be free from his pew imprisonment.

Warily, I let him past to explore the aisle. He's a wanderer, though, and I'm no rookie, so I stood too, bouncing our newborn and keeping watch. Sure enough, it only took him a minute to meander away. I knew if he rounded the front pew and spotted his beloved big sister, all bets would be off, so I hastily called him back.

"Augustine!" I whisper-yelled. He stopped in his tracks, and slowly turned his head to look at me, a mischievous grin on his face.

"Augustine," I called again, my face a mask of displeasure, my voice rebuking him. He didn't continue forward, but neither did he come back. He just grinned at me, then looked back over his shoulder toward freedom.

Suddenly, I realized my anger was going to send him running. Inspired by the crucifix behind him, I squatted down and opened my arms wide, a look of love on my face. Without the need for another word, my sweet boy ran toward me and threw himself into my arms.

In that moment, I knew I had turned a corner in my parenting, and perhaps one in my relationship with my Eternal Father, as well.

As a mother, I have to set limits for my son's safety without wavering, or he won't take me seriously, but in order to draw him back, I must offer love and affection. Isn't that how God works, too? He doesn't mince words, because he knows what's best for us, but he also lovingly seeks us whenever we stray, and he rejoices in our return.

This selection from Romans might feel harsh to us. God is calling us away from our sins, and he does us the great service of clearly spelling some of them out, as well as the consequences those sins will bring. In other words, he sets before us firm boundaries that we must not cross. He isn't a tyrannical or capricious God, though. Unity with him is what makes us whole, and we can't accomplish that wholeness when we are mired in sin.

Why then, in this selection from St. Paul to the Romans, do we read not once, not twice, but three times that "God gave them up"? Does that mean that God despaired of his sinful children? That he shrugged his shoulders and walked away from them?

No. Our God will never abandon us. However, because his love is total and complete, he respects our free will. God will not force himself upon us; rather, he will allow us to choose him freely, even if that means choosing sin.

What, then, are we to make of God's anger in this passage?

God's anger here isn't directed at us. It's focused on the sin in our lives, and his "holy hostility" is on our behalf! He sent his only Son, Jesus Christ, to take the punishment due to us from our sinfulness! Our heavenly Father longs for us to stop at the boundaries he has set and to turn around, to see in his divine gaze the love he has for us.

Will you stop when God tells you to stop? Will you see clearly the death and destruction that lie before you if you continue on the path of sin, and will you turn around and make your way back into his loving embrace?

How do we do accomplish such a daunting task? The answer is always to look to the cross, and then to the resurrection. A God who can do such mighty deeds, who loves us with such wild abandon, surely will welcome us back when we come to him with contrite hearts.

So, what are you waiting for?

Micaela Darr

The wrath of God toward sin that Paul addresses in this section can feel harsh. It is important to address that God's holy hostility is not at us, but for us. That hostility is provoked by his love of us and is the impetus for the mercy that saves us. How do you recognize your own sin and trust in God's mercy knowing how your sin has grieved his heart?

OPEN YOUR BIBLE

ROMANS
CHAPTER 2

SCRIPTURE NOTES:

Focus Verse

All who have sinned apart from the law will also perish apart from the law, and all who have sinned under the law will be judged by the law. For it is not the hearers of the law who are righteous in God's sight, but the doers of the law who will be justified.

Romans 2:12-13

FOR FURTHER READING:
Matthew 7:21-23

CONSIDER THE COMPONENTS OF LECTIO DIVINA

read	*meditate*
pray	*contemplate*

Day Four

You want to know the good news? This is it: We are born sinners, dead in our sin, and God so wants to save us that he came into the world to live a perfectly holy life and to die in our place so that we could trust him with our eternal life. He came to free us and he wants us to be free.

That's the good news. But we have a tendency to mess it up.

We have to give our assent. We have to want to be his people. We have to turn away from sin and towards his patient kindness.

We can't free ourselves from the bondage of sin and we can't open for ourselves the gates of heaven. Holiness is what God accomplished for us and he gives us the grace necessary to become holy as he is holy—if we open ourselves to him in faith. With the gift of his Son on the cross, God frees us to live an abundant life in his grace, if only we stop struggling to accomplish it all on our own and trust him to deliver us.

We have all sinned and fallen short of the glory of God (Romans 3:23), even the Jewish people, who have seen God's favor throughout the Old Testament. Not one of us has managed to live in perfect obedience to the Lord. St. Paul calls us up short here and begs us to consider that every single one of us is proud and rebellious and mortally flawed. Every one of us needs Christ to live.

But not many people are willing to admit that, deep down inside, they are really sinful, and therefore separated from God and in need of what the Bible calls salvation. Surely, most of us have no problem identifying sin, and as we consult the last few verses of the first chapter of Romans for a list of sins, we recognize all of them. But with such a list in hand, most of us will more readily identify sin in other people than we will in ourselves.

St. Paul insists we see the hypocrisy in our judgment. Our lives depend on it. He tells us that we have no excuse and we must condemn ourselves. Further, a good God who is rich in kindness gave his very life so that we would recognize our sin and amend our lives before the day of wrath when he comes in righteous judgment. This God? This being who created us and will come again to judge us? He is kind and good, and his kindness is meant to lead us to repentance.

God pours out this kindness in abundance—it is rich and flowing. And it is patient. God is very patient with us, leading us to him with forbearance, despite our stubborn resistance. This gives us real hope, both for ourselves and for those we love. God will not give up; he will not forsake us. Until we draw our last breath, he will call us to himself.

God doesn't settle for the rote and ritualistic offering of adhering to the letter of the law. Jesus' frequent cautions to the Pharisees in the gospels call out especially to those of us who know our theology and practice our religion. It's no mistake that God gave us St. Paul, who looks at Christ with incredible love through the lens of someone who was once a Pharisee himself (Acts 23:6).

Paul addresses this reality when he speaks to the Jewish custom of circumcision and contrasts it with "real circumcision" (v.29). Real circumcision isn't a physical religious ritual; it's the peeling back of the layers of my heart so that what truly lies there is revealed. Real circumcision isn't for God. It's for me. It's the first step in confronting my own sin in an honest way and then repenting. After that kind of exposure before the Lord, he is able to enter into my heart and to redeem my soul by his mercy and grace.

Elizabeth Foss

Paul here addresses both judging one another and relying on compliance to the moral law for our salvation. He points us back to the truth that it is only by love and through love that we can be saved. It is God's love that animates us and gives us spiritual life, and does the same for everyone else we encounter. How does seeing yourself and your spiritual life through the lens of unearned love affect the way you see others?

OPEN YOUR BIBLE

ROMANS
CHAPTER 3

SCRIPTURE NOTES:

Focus Verse

...since all have sinned and fall short of
the glory of God; they are now justified
by his grace as a gift, through the
redemption that is in Christ Jesus...

Romans 3:23-24

FOR FURTHER READING:
Psalm 14:1-3
Psalm 53:1-3

CONSIDER THE COMPONENTS OF LECTIO DIVINA

read	*meditate*
pray	*contemplate*

Day Five

Although I was born and raised Catholic, it wasn't until college that I began to grasp the importance of maintaining a strong interior life, which, for me, meant making the effort to attend daily Mass, frequent confession, holy hours during the week, and to do Bible reading and spend time in prayer every day.

When I became a mother, however, most of these things went out the window.

I married a year after graduation, and over the next six years, my husband and I were blessed with four little ones who arrived like clockwork every twenty months or so. Between the children's inconsistent schedules, and the physical and mental drain of pregnancy and childcare, the time and energy that I used to give to my prayer life vanished quickly.

After our fourth child was born, my mornings looked something like this: Bleary-eyed from a night of interrupted sleep, I would be up before the sun with my early-rising toddlers, sitting in the midst of the toys I forgot to clean the night before and feeling the nausea that comes from an ever-growing sleep deficit. While the toddlers narrated their play to me and I nursed the baby, I would feel nothing but how entirely exhausted I was. I had no idea how on earth I would make it to lunch, let alone to the end of the day. The thought would cross my mind to stop, grab my Bible, and do five minutes of mental prayer, but I would resist. I was too tired to pray, prayer felt too hard and would take too much effort, and I had nothing left. By noon, I would have lost my temper with each child multiple times, and by the time I got the littlest ones in their beds for naps, my own guilt-ridden tears would have started. My sins of the morning would replay in my head like a terrible movie, and I would feel sure God wanted nothing to do with me.

It was around this time that I began meeting regularly with a spiritual mentor who encouraged me to revisit how I thought of God and of meeting him in prayer. I had assumed that prayer was something I did, hinging on my own efforts, and that my standing with God depended on these efforts that I no longer felt capable of making. What this spiritual mentor helped me to see is that God's love always comes first. Prayer is first and foremost an acknowledgement that I am in God's loving presence. This paradigm of prayer in fact fits beautifully and far more easily into my vocation as a wife and mother: small prayers throughout the day telling our Lord that I know that he is with me, that he sees me, that he hears me, and that he loves me. These prayers began to transform my life, and over time they have made it much easier to enter into more extended mental prayer when less-crazy seasons of life have allowed for it.

St. Paul says in Romans 3, "Since all have sinned and fall short of the glory of God; they are now justified by his grace as a gift, through the redemption that is in Christ Jesus." (Romans 3:23-24) Our Lord has already accomplished the work of my salvation, and what he is asking of me is not to work for this myself, but to say "yes" daily to him and to what he is accomplishing in me. To be sure, this requires effort, but my efforts are not what win God's ever-present love for me. That love, and his grace, are his gift. In return, he is not looking for set prayers that I can cross off a checklist, but for my heart. God's grace is not hindered by my fatigue or my weakness, for it is in these very things that he manifests his great power and mercy. (2 Corinthians 12:9)

Ana Hahn

In order to fully experience God's love for us, we have to be willing to accept how desperately we need that love, and have faith that his love is enough to do what we cannot do for ourselves: save ourselves from sin. In what ways does your own desperate need for God draw you closer to him?

OPEN YOUR BIBLE

ROMANS
CHAPTER 4

SCRIPTURE NOTES:

Focus Verse

For the promise that he would inherit
the world did not come to Abraham
or to his descendants through the law
but through the righteousness of faith...
He did not weaken in faith when he
considered his own body, which was
already as good as dead (for he was
about a hundred years old), or when he
considered the barrenness of Sarah's
womb. No distrust made him waver
concerning the promise of God, but he
grew strong in his faith as he gave glory
to God, being fully convinced that God
was able to do what he had promised.
Therefore his faith "was reckoned to him
as righteousness."
Romans 4:13, 19-22

FOR FURTHER READING:
Galatians 3:19-22

CONSIDER THE COMPONENTS OF LECTIO DIVINA

read	*meditate*
pray	*contemplate*

Day Six

The walk was well over a mile and we hadn't slept much in the past thirty-six hours, but you would never know it. Our four-year-old marched along, skipping and singing happily, as we inched ever closer to the spot she had been dreaming of for much of her short four years on this earth.

After we finally ascended the many stairs, she sat down at the top of the Trocadero gazing across the plaza at the soaring *Tour Eiffel* standing stately in the park. I sat down next to her on the stair and she gently rested her head on my shoulder, letting out a contented sigh. She couldn't take her eyes off of the tower, her hope now a living reality.

Less than a year prior, she began to add a finishing flourish to our evening prayer that began with, "St. Joan of Arc, help us get to France…" A lovely, whimsical wish, my husband and I both thought, as we didn't see a trip there feasible any time in the near future.

She had developed this love for France, particularly embodied in the Eiffel Tower, from the time she could talk, admittedly inherited and stirred by my own love for the country. Upon learning a bit about the meek and mighty saint from a little French town who led the entire French army in a winning war against the English, she took St. Joan as her own in winning the fight of all things working against her to make a trip to France.

God had placed this desire on my daughter's heart and she was determined to see it through. Every night, without fail, she offered up this uncomplicated prayer that she had composed. In hope she believed against hope, like Abraham, that her desire was not in vain. The near impossibility of a trip actually happening did not disrupt her faith.

A trip to the East Coast was planned in the autumn. Often, when we make such a grand, cross-country trip, we attempt to add another place to the agenda in relative close proximity to make the most of the haul it takes to get there. We had our sights set on an excursion in Maine to see the spectacular fall foliage, but each itinerary we tried to put together kept showing up with a roadblock. The hotel was closing down for the season the week prior and there was no method of easily accessible transportation to a particular island, among other stumbling blocks. Discouragement was creeping in, and I called my husband at work to let him know that Maine didn't seem viable after all.

As soon as we hung up, on a whim, I hopped over to the travel search engine and typed in "Virginia to Paris". Wouldn't you know, the tickets there were nearly the same price as the trip to Maine? When my husband walked in the door that evening, I sprang on him the news that I discovered, and he shared that he had done exactly the same when we got off the phone earlier. Perhaps it was time to go to France?

There was no following of the perfect formula, arranging our lives just so. It was all grace. It was all gift. As it unfolded, I could only stand in awe of my daughter's faith. Her simple prayer, a petition to God, a response to the desire in her heart.

It is utterly this straightforward walking in faith, walking in his grace. We imagine there to be so many hoops we must jump through to be in God's good graces, to merit his love. Rather, it is given without warrant.

Like Abraham, like my child, we are called forth to walk with him in faith. In the big, in the small, in the daily humdrum, in the grand adventure. Rest on his grace.

Laurel Muff

In this chapter, Paul focuses on Abraham as an example of righteousness. Abraham would be a familiar figure for the Jewish converts reading this letter, and an example of faith who has been set before them all their lives. It is Abraham's faith in God that is credited to him as righteousness, not his spiritual perfection. It is God who is glorified in Abraham's story of faith, not Abraham. How do you remind yourself that it is God's story we see played out in the lives of our spiritual heroes, not their own perfection?

Savor

Charcuterie

INGREDIENTS FOR THE ULTIMATE CHARCUTERIE

fresh figs	prosciutto
grapes	hummus
blueberries	manchego cheese
dried apricots	brie cheese
dates	fresh mozzarella cheese
olives	goat cheese
roasted red peppers	bread or crackers
sard salami	

THE ART OF CHARCUTERIE

While a charcuterie board looks exceptionally pretty and sometimes even a little (or a lot) fancy, it's actually a very easy hostess trick. Combine a variety of textures and flavors, let yourself enjoy the act of "designing" the tray (play with your food), and know that nothing is against the rules because there are no rules.

Creating the tray should be fun! When it comes to slicing meats, consider buying them pre-sliced to save you time and aggravation. While you're there, check your deli section (and places likes Costco) for fun things to inspire you, like meats already wrapped around cheeses, and little jars of mustard or special jam or spiced nuts. If you slice the meat yourself, be sure the meat is cold to slice. Slice as thinly as you can. When you lay it on the tray, consider rolling or folding to add depth to the presentation. Then, serve it at room temperature.

A charcuterie board is art; it's different every time and everyone brings her own touch to it. Yours will be just right for you.

flourish

a day for Selah

Use this day for pause, prayer, praise, and rest.

Day Eight

Memory
VERSE

Week Two

And not only that, but we also boast in our
sufferings, knowing that suffering produces
endurance, and endurance produces
character, and character produces hope,
and hope does not disappoint us, because
God's love has been poured into our hearts
through the Holy Spirit that has been
given to us.

ROMANS 5:3-5

I will practice Scripture memory by:
- ○ Praying
- ○ Writing
- ○ Speaking
- ○ Reading
- ○ Other: _____

God's love has been poured into our hearts through the Holy Spirit

ROMANS 5:5

OPEN YOUR BIBLE

ROMANS
CHAPTER 5

SCRIPTURE NOTES:

Focus Verse

And the free gift is not like the effect of the one man's sin. For the judgment following one trespass brought condemnation, but the free gift following many trespasses brings justification. If, because of the one man's trespass, death exercised dominion through that one, much more surely will those who receive the abundance of grace and the free gift of righteousness exercise dominion in life through the one man, Jesus Christ. Therefore just as one man's trespass led to condemnation for all, so one man's act of righteousness leads to justification and life for all. For just as by the one man's disobedience the many were made sinners, so by the one man's obedience the many will be made righteous. But law came in, with the result that the trespass multiplied; but where sin increased, grace abounded all the more, so that, just as sin exercised dominion in death, so grace might also exercise dominion through justification leading to eternal life through Jesus Christ our Lord.

Romans 5:16-21

FOR FURTHER READING:
Philippians 4:19
2 Corinthians 5:21
Ephesians 2:8-10

CONSIDER THE COMPONENTS OF LECTIO DIVINA

read	*meditate*
pray	*contemplate*

Day Nine

It was a summer of dying—and of rebirth. I kind of staggered into it, plodding along through April and May, my usual serious and diligent self, always busy and always productive. And then there was June. The deadlines got moved up, the workload doubled. I dug deep. I rearranged the calendar. I made more checklists. I checked off every item on them. I even uttered the words out loud: Spiritual warfare won't get me now. We're all buttoned up here. I'm exhausted, but I'm accomplished. All is well.

And then it hit. An emotional storm like none I'd ever experienced. A fight for the well-being of my child that I'd never in a million years anticipated. A crisis in my Church that had eerie parallels to the crisis as parents we'd been asked to endure, to the cause we'd newly been expected to champion.

I was the person with the perfectly checked-off checklist. And suddenly, the things being thrust upon me defied being written in tidy rows. The watershed moment of my motherhood was demanding more of me than I could summon from the depths of my type-A, ultra-efficient self.

I fell apart. I couldn't eat. I couldn't sleep. I became more and more exhausted and frantic. What was this mission God gave me that I could not possibly do? Why would he assign such a thing? I've always been quick to answer the call, always told myself I could do hard things for God. Suddenly, I could do nothing. I moved numbly from day to day, and just barely prayed that nothing else would need me.

Things began to spin out of control: details forgotten, careless mistakes, arguments that sprung from a place of deep depletion and even despair. And then, one day, I woke up with a full to-do list and I muscled through. I wondered why I felt so "off." I wondered why my watch kept alerting me that my heart rate was too high even at rest. I wondered why the July day was so very cold. And by 8:00 that night, I wondered if I should take my temperature.

I had a raging fever.

For the next three days, I stayed in bed. I cried a lot. I prayed a lot. And I tossed and turned. A lot. In the middle of the third night, I gave up. I told God that I'd worked super hard for him and there was nothing I wouldn't do for him, but I was really in over my head this time and I was very sorry I wasn't up to the task, but I had to resign from this particular life of service. I wasn't up to the job.

I surrendered. It was the only thing left to do.

And there he was—in my suffering. I could almost hear him say, "I thought you'd never ask. This is not—nor has it ever been—about what you can do." With the dawn, I felt strength in the new day, not the familiar fatigue that usually came with poor sleep. I had conversations that were incredibly fruitful and healing, that truly astonish me in their mercy and grace even now as I recall them. That hot night as August met July is the night I surrendered and let myself fall into God's tender care without holding anything in reserve as work to do by myself.

The work? The work to which I'd become a slave because I had to prove how much I love him by doing and doing and doing? God has already done it. To the gift of faith, he has added the extravagant gift of grace. That grace allowed me to surrender, and surrender gave me hope again.

It's not all rainbows and unicorns.

It is true that I have suffered for Christ, and there will be more suffering. But I reached a crossroads where I could choose to try to continue on under my own strength—strength I had depleted—or I could endure in nothing but hope. Hope held the future. Would I open myself to his grace and allow him to give me reason to hope?

Yes. At the end of myself, because of the gift of faith, I would.

I did.

Quiet hope began to light the darkest corners of my despair.

Salvation—my own, my family's, the Church's—does not depend on my ability to get things done for God as though he needs my help. He has already won salvation. But my peace in this broken, fallen world, where evil lurks and threatens everything I hold dear, depends on my ability to surrender to his tenderness and let him pour love directly into my heart. That love lets me live empowered, despite my very human weakness. That love is—quite literally— everything.

Elizabeth Foss

After guiding the Romans to grapple with the reality of their sinfulness and need for redemption in the chapters before this, Romans 5 is a chapter on the hope of eternal life and the value of pursuing it. It is the happy ending to the story of our sin. Where can you see hope amid the ashes of your life? How does the reality of eternal life change the way you live your earthly life?

OPEN YOUR BIBLE

ROMANS
CHAPTER 6

SCRIPTURE NOTES:

Focus Verse

What then are we to say? Should we continue in sin in order that grace may abound? By no means! How can we who died to sin go on living in it? Do you not know that all of us who have been baptized into Christ Jesus were baptized into his death? Therefore we have been buried with him by baptism into death, so that, just as Christ was raised from the dead by the glory of the Father, so we too might walk in newness of life. For if we have been united with him in a death like his, we will certainly be united with him in a resurrection like his. We know that our old self was crucified with him so that the body of sin might be destroyed, and we might no longer be enslaved to sin. For whoever has died is freed from sin. But if we have died with Christ, we believe that we will also live with him. We know that Christ, being raised from the dead, will never die again; death no longer has dominion over him. The death he died, he died to sin, once for all; but the life he lives, he lives to God. So you also must consider yourselves dead to sin and alive to God in Christ Jesus.

Romans 6:1-11

FOR FURTHER READING:
2 Corinthians 5:16-21

CONSIDER THE COMPONENTS OF LECTIO DIVINA

read	*meditate*
pray	*contemplate*

Day Ten

In 1999, I had a profound experience that led me back to the faith of my childhood. I'd been an arrogant and foolish young adult, traveling down a destructive path of my own design, believing I was "liberated" and "alive" when, in truth, I was enslaved by my passions and dead in my sin.

One night, I lay awake in a sweltering hotel room in eastern Oregon, feeling completely broken and defeated. In that seemingly godforsaken place, I cried out to the Lord from the depths of my soul. While it would take pages to explain exactly what happened in that moment, suffice it to say I finally knew that God could have mercy on me, that Jesus died for my sins, and that by his sacrifice I could leave my sin and guilt at the foot of the cross. I didn't have to just survive; in the amazing grace bought by his precious blood on Calvary, I could flourish.

I quickly realized that, if I desired to, as St. Paul wrote, "walk in newness of life," (Romans 6:4) I had to make some—okay, many—big changes. While I would love to tell you that my life looked completely different after that incredibly restless night—that I did a 180, completely cleaned up my act, changed my tune—that's not exactly how my prodigal story unfolded. It has taken a lot of prayer, meditation, sacramental graces, and an ocean of divine mercy to put my former ways to death so that I am (mostly) no longer enslaved to sin. (Romans 6:6)

I say "mostly," because a crucial component of my faith journey involved realizing that, although I'd chosen to follow the narrow way again, I would still wrestle with my fallen nature. Even to this day, as I lean on God's boundless mercy and sanctifying grace, I often stumble and fall short. I lose my temper and lash out at those I am called to love. I neglect personal prayer yet find time to scroll through social media. I consume calories I don't need, watch shows I shouldn't watch, and purchase material goods I can't afford.

Here's a poorly kept secret: I sin in spite of myself. As it turns out, I am human. I'm incapable of redeeming myself. And as someone who wants to be in control, that's frustrating. Maybe you can relate.

The glorious good news for all of us is that sin isn't entitled to the final word in our lives. We can, according to St. Paul, "yield our members to righteousness for sanctification." (Romans 6:20) We can choose to put our selfish desires and sinful tendencies to death, uniting our sacrifices and suffering to Christ's ultimate sacrifice on the cross. In this way, we grow in holiness, experiencing an incredible foretaste of the abundant life that only Jesus can give. Death no longer has power over us, and we are resurrected—set free.

For me, being alive in Christ and dead to sin is worlds away from how I lived before this conversion. As a wife of seventeen years and mother of five beautifully challenging souls, I can attest that there are hundreds of ways I can choose love, Christ, and holiness. There are even more ways I can choose pride, anger, and selfishness. It is up to me to decide.

The path to holiness is rarely easy; there are many pitfalls, and I often fall short. But marriage and family life is my path to sanctification. It is my call to love. It is my call to eternal life, a gift freely given by the grace of God—if only I turn and follow him.

Heather Renshaw

The reality is that the good news of the resurrection and our hope of eternal life won by God's generous grace still doesn't free us from our concupiscence and tendency to sin. Holiness is a thousand little deaths to self daily, which bring us into the sufferings of Christ and give us a part of his resurrection. What does it look like for you to live dead to sin and alive in Christ?

OPEN YOUR BIBLE

ROMANS

CHAPTER 7

SCRIPTURE NOTES:

Focus Verse

I do not understand my own actions. For I do not do what I want, but I do the very thing I hate. Now if I do what I do not want, I agree that the law is good. But in fact it is no longer I that do it, but sin that dwells within me. For I know that nothing good dwells within me, that is, in my flesh. I can will what is right, but I cannot do it. For I do not do the good I want, but the evil I do not want is what I do. Now if I do what I do not want, it is no longer I that do it, but sin that dwells within me.

Romans 7:15-20

FOR FURTHER READING:

1 Corinthians 15:56-58

CONSIDER THE COMPONENTS OF LECTIO DIVINA

read	*meditate*
pray	*contemplate*

Day Eleven

Too often, I end the day longing to fall asleep, but unable to stop speaking words of disgust to myself that I would never, ever speak to someone else. This unhealthy practice is one I return to whenever I succumb to a well-worn pattern of sin—a pattern I've tried to overcome for years. I hate this sin and want nothing more than to leave it in my past, but I find myself repeating it and confessing it again and again. And each time, I'm a little more disappointed in myself.

The struggle to overcome the sins we despise as we strive to obey and honor the God that we love is universal. Can't we all recall times when, like Paul, we too could say, "For I do not do what I want, but I do the very thing I hate"? (Romans 7:15) And even when we long to do God's will with our whole hearts, the weakness of our flesh often causes us to struggle despite our best intentions. Even when the Holy Spirit has strengthened us to do God's will through baptism and confirmation, we're still not immune to temptation or sin.

God calls us to invite him into our struggle and ask for his forgiveness and strength so that we might have hope of ending the pattern. But that's much easier said than done, because for many of us, it's hard to stop trying to overcome these sins on our own. Our pride blinds us, making us mistakenly believe that the desire to stop these patterns of sin is enough. We don't fully recognize or acknowledge the weakness of our flesh, so we don't truly comprehend how greatly we need God. Instead, we stubbornly try to overcome these habitual sins on our own, and each time we fail, we move dangerously closer to giving up.

On a recent once-in-a-lifetime trip to Italy, amidst the break in my routine, I could finally see the hold the habitual sin I've been struggling with for many years has on me in my everyday life. And as I prayed one morning, it suddenly dawned on me that, in my stubbornness and pride, I've never really admitted to myself or to God how deeply I need him to help me overcome this pattern. The sun was shining through the stained-glass windows of the chapel, bathing the wooden pews in vibrant color, and in that warm, holy place, seemingly aglow with God's merciful love, I finally asked him to step in and help me carry a cross that I was never meant to carry alone.

Despite this breakthrough, I haven't ended this pattern of sin completely, and perhaps I never will. But by inviting God into the struggle, I have a renewed sense of hope. And each time I've succumbed to this sin since then, it's gotten easier and easier to turn to the words of prayer instead of self-loathing.

As Christians, we are people made new, filled with the Spirit of Christ. And yet, we continue to inhabit bodies that are susceptible to sin. But rather than letting that truth lead us to despair, may we let it be the reminder we need to stay alert and keep fighting the inclinations toward sin that threaten to derail us. And through it all, let us remember that we have already been set free from the bondage of sin by Christ. That is the reason we can live in hopefulness, and where we can draw the strength we need to get up again when we fail, ready to try again, with Christ at our side.

Allison McGinley

Paul's frustration with his own sin and his inability to consistently follow God with his body as he mentally wants to is a frustration we all know. Sin is the human condition. We all want to follow God perfectly, but none of us does. But God gave us a remedy in the person of Christ and the life we have in the Spirit. How does it look for you to approach the reality of your sinful condition and hold on to the truth that Christ has set you free from being captive to that sin?

OPEN YOUR BIBLE

ROMANS
8:1-17

SCRIPTURE NOTES:

Focus Verse

So then, brothers and sisters, we are debtors, not to the flesh, to live according to the flesh—for if you live according to the flesh, you will die; but if by the Spirit you put to death the deeds of the body, you will live. For all who are led by the Spirit of God are children of God. For you did not receive a spirit of slavery to fall back into fear, but you have received a spirit of adoption. When we cry, "Abba! Father!" it is that very Spirit bearing witness with our spirit that we are children of God, and if children, then heirs, heirs of God and joint heirs with Christ—if, in fact, we suffer with him so that we may also be glorified with him.

Romans 8:12-17

FOR FURTHER READING:

Colossians 3:5-10

CONSIDER THE COMPONENTS OF LECTIO DIVINA

read	*meditate*
pray	*contemplate*

Day Twelve

My brother Josh is the greatest father. He's always playing with four-year-old Ellyn, and she delights in her daddy.

I watched recently as the two of them enjoyed what they call the "froggy game." Ellyn crouched low and then hopped, and Josh caught her mid-air and then effortlessly tossed her high above his head.

The well-developed, frontal lobe part of me that prudently assesses risk panicked each time Ellyn's small body started to free fall. What if he didn't catch her, and she somehow fell through a canyon created by his outstretched arms? But from Ellyn's peals of laughter and constant petitions for "More!", it was clear my niece harbored no such fear. Her daddy had never let her down before. Why should this moment be any different?

Ellyn has a complete, childlike trust in her father.

> In God, whose word I praise,
> in God I trust; I am not afraid;
> what can flesh do to me?
> (Psalm 56:4-5)

Young children trust so well. They naturally look outside of themselves—and the big, scary world—for comfort.

They're quick to believe and aren't bogged down by years of doubts and disappointments. They have an easier time accepting the love gifted to them without questioning if they're really worthy. They ask questions, and they trust the answers even if they don't completely make sense. Then our children grow older, and while their daddy may have always caught them during the froggy game, they've fallen in other ways, sometimes through their own sins and failings, and sometimes through absolutely no fault of their own.

And that beautiful childlike faith may begin to wither. It has, at times, for me. I've often been more childish than childlike in my faith. I make demands of God. *Convert this loved one. Then I'll know you really love me. Help me to never sin again. Then I'll know you're truly the ruler of my heart.* Or, *this suffering doesn't make sense. Nothing makes sense. I'm not sure I can trust in you or your plan for me.*

So I turn away from my Father. I'm convinced he's not going to be there to catch me when I stumble and when life gets rough. My heart is hurting, longing, and I've wrongly believed that something rather than someone would fulfill me.

A child looks first to her parents for comfort and love, but we frequently turn to the outside world to fill the God-shaped hole in our hearts. Maybe we convince ourselves when we lose those last fifteen pounds, get that much-deserved promotion, or finally conceive the baby we've been aching to hold, we will flourish.

Yet we remain stuck in the wake of the suffering that life inevitably dishes out, and in our own inability to make things happen. Meanwhile, Abba, our own daddy, invites us to call out to him when we're confused, sad, scared, or paralyzed by sin. My friends, I know all too well the heavy burden of sin. I've felt incapable of turning to my Father for mercy. Sometimes I've felt as if God has abandoned me. Unlike my niece, I've slipped through his arms.

Or so I thought.

Looking back, I see now that God's love and mercy weren't only gifts I received when I returned to him; they were always there for me. It was, in fact, his very mercy that inspired me to turn back to him in the first place.

God seeks you out every single day. Just as you are. You don't have to be perfect to receive his love. You don't have to eliminate every sinful impulse to experience the peace of Christ. You just have to try. All we have to do is welcome Jesus into our hearts and try (again and again) to trust and surrender to our Abba.

Kate Wicker

The "Abba Father" verse in this section is often cited when we speak of God's love for us and our response to that love. In this point of the letter to the Romans, it's a great relief. After digging into the painful condition of our sinfulness, we are finally presented with the remedy our hearts long for—that Christ redeems us and we are children of God. How does being God's daughter affect the way you see yourself and the way you live in this world and respond to others?

OPEN YOUR BIBLE

ROMANS
8:18-39

SCRIPTURE NOTES:

Focus Verse

What then are we to say about these things? If God is for us, who is against us? He who did not withhold his own Son, but gave him up for all of us, will he not with him also give us everything else? Who will bring any charge against God's elect? It is God who justifies. Who is to condemn? It is Christ Jesus, who died, yes, who was raised, who is at the right hand of God, who indeed intercedes for us. Who will separate us from the love of Christ? Will hardship, or distress, or persecution, or famine, or nakedness, or peril, or sword? As it is written,

"For your sake we are being killed all day long;
we are accounted as sheep to be slaughtered."

No, in all these things we are more than conquerors through him who loved us. For I am convinced that neither death, nor life, nor angels, nor rulers, nor things present, nor things to come, nor powers, nor height, nor depth, nor anything else in all creation, will be able to separate us from the love of God in Christ Jesus our Lord.

Romans 8:31-39

FOR FURTHER READING:
2 Corinthians 5:6-10

CONSIDER THE COMPONENTS OF LECTIO DIVINA

read	*meditate*
pray	*contemplate*

Day Thirteen

We were hunched over, chins on our knuckles, staring with the passionate intensity that only a middle school basketball game can bring. The gym was too quiet; I was used to watching games where Dad verbally coached every move with a clipboard in hand and a pen behind his ear: "Stick to your man!" "That's all right, girls, back on D!" "Hustle, dribble, move that ball!" He made efforts not to be so vocal (they were only kids, after all) by sucking on lollipops during games, but the garbled suggestions would find a way out anyway, and a chewed-apart mess of candy would end up behind his ear instead of the pen. This was the first game since Dad had passed, and a new, much quieter coach was leading the charge. The gym was silent except for the kids' sneakers, the dribble of the ball, and an occasional golf-clap response to some action.

And then my sister snatched the ball away from the person she was defending.

My other sister, Gaby, had always been the most refined crowd member and therefore the most embarrassed by the loud displays from the family. But as soon as Becky touched the ball, I heard a scream from the seat next to me echo around the gym: "YES BECKY, GO! THIS IS YOUR MOMENT!"

Becky nearly tripped from laughing as she dribbled the ball down the court, and the crowd of families laughed with her. We siblings became more annoying after that, heckling her from the stands, not filling Dad's shoes but not leaving them empty, either: "You go, girl!" "Dribble, hon-NEY, dribble!" "That was terrible, but that's okay, you tried!" And when she finally made a basket, we screamed, making far too much of a fuss, and causing Becky to look back at us, mildly annoyed, but laughing all the same.

In the end, I think they lost. It didn't matter. My sweet youngest sister was in the thick of it, emotionally and physically: twelve years old without a dad to coach her to the end of her basketball season, and, to top it off, nothing seemed to be going right in the game. She needed a cheering squad.

I want you to take a second and look at your game right now, and acknowledge that parts of it are really tough. Too often, it's hard enough to keep going, let alone to keep the energy up. In times like these, you might be in need of a good pep talk.

One of my father's most-quoted verses was Romans 8:31: "If God is for us, who can be against us?"

Guys, those are such great odds.

In the game of life, God cheers loudly for you in the stands, especially if you feel like you're losing. Although 8:31 is the cornerstone, I challenge you to read the sentence in verses 38 and 39 aloud. There should be a movie soundtrack building to a soaring crescendo behind these words; this is Paul's inspirational speech before we go off to battle.

Read it aloud, okay? Don't be shy:

> For I am convinced that neither death, nor life, nor angels, nor rulers, nor things present, nor things to come, nor powers, nor height, nor depth, nor anything else in all creation, will be able to separate us from the love of God in Christ Jesus our Lord.

BOOM, baby. God loves you, and because God is for you, who can be against you? You can do anything good. Those hard parts of your game that you were thinking about earlier are still very hard. But you've got this because God's got this. I don't believe that what doesn't kill you makes you stronger, but it can, and often does, make you. Show 'em what you're made of. Truly, you can do this. I wish I could cheer for you from the stands like my sister did, but pretend you just got the ball and I'm screaming for you now: GO, SISTER! THIS IS YOUR MOMENT!

All right team, let's make it a great day, on three—

One, two, three: GREAT DAY.

Katy Greiner

The great joy of being a child of God, as we are identified in the beginning of chapter eight of Romans, is that we are known by him. He knows the words we cannot speak. He knows the words we cannot pray. He hears his own Spirit crying out to him on our behalf. And because of this, we are never far from him. Even when life's hardships make it seem God is distant, he is ever near to the ones he loves. How do you remind yourself that God sees you and knows you and wants to draw close to you when life is hard and it seems God is far away?

Savor

Classic Marinara

INGREDIENTS

7-10 garlic cloves

3 tbsp virgin olive oil

2 15 oz cans of peeled whole

tomatoes

salt and pepper to taste

fresh basil

DIRECTIONS

Saute 7-10 cloves of fresh garlic in extra virgin olive oil until not quite golden. (It's important never to brown the garlic.)

Add two cans of imported whole tomatoes or preferably fresh peeled tomatoes (a must in the summer when they are abundant). Mash the tomatoes slightly with a fork, as this sauce should be chunky.

Add seasoning: salt, pepper, and of course lots of fresh chopped basil.

Simmer uncovered for 25 minutes.

Serve over your favorite pasta.

flourish

a day for Selah

Use this day for pause, prayer, praise, and rest.

Day Fifteen

Memory

V E R S E

Week Three

As it is written, "How beautiful are the
feet of those who bring good news!" But
not all have obeyed the good news; for
Isaiah says, "Lord, who has believed our
message?" So faith comes from what is
heard, and what is heard comes through
the word of Christ.

ROMANS 10:16-17

I will practice Scripture memory by:

○ Praying

○ Writing

○ Speaking

○ Reading

○ Other: _____

ROMANS 10:17

OPEN YOUR BIBLE

ROMANS
CHAPTER 9

SCRIPTURE NOTES:

Focus Verse

What then are we to say? Is there injustice on God's part? By no means! For he says to Moses,
"I will have mercy on whom I have mercy, and I will have compassion on whom I have compassion."
So it depends not on human will or exertion, but on God who shows mercy.
Romans 9:14-16

FOR FURTHER READING:
Matthew 11:27

CONSIDER THE COMPONENTS OF LECTIO DIVINA

read	*meditate*
pray	*contemplate*

Day Sixteen

"I will have mercy on whom I have mercy,
and I will have compassion on whom I have compassion."
(Romans 9:15)

"…and no one knows the Father except the Son and any one to whom the Son chooses to reveal him." (Matthew 11:27)

These are verses that keep me awake at night.

To live the Christian life for any length of time is to wonder, "Why me?" and "What is to become of him?" Why has God shown compassion on me? Why has he infused me with faith and instilled in me a strong sense that a life grounded in him is rich with hope? Why does this favor not fall on everyone in my family? In my neighborhood?

From the vantage point of one who has come to know God's gratuitous mercy, it is especially painful to watch loved ones struggle and to understand that God could rescue them, that he could have compassion on them and they would be delivered from the curse of being cut off from Christ (Romans 9:3). They could have boundless mercy.

But they don't.

Does God keep himself from them?

He doesn't. Jesus' whole life here on earth was about revealing God to his people. God wants us—all of us—for himself. St. Paul understands this, and he is heartbroken over those who are not yet reached by the living Lord. Paul has been transformed by the gospel and he is so grateful and so on fire for Jesus. His joy in his own redemption is colored by his enormous sorrow as he grapples with his own questions about why God's ways of salvation are so mysterious and, honestly, so often troubling. With St. Paul, we consider the sorrow that comes from knowing that people we love can and do rebel, or close their eyes to his goodness, or choose to harden their hearts to his mercy.

The reality of God can be hidden from them because they lack the humility to acknowledge that, without God, they are nothing. They keep trying to be the lord of their own lives. Cardinal Ratzinger describes it this way:

> The greater a being is, the more it wants to determine its own life. It wants to be less and less dependent and, thus, more and more itself a kind of god, needing no one else at all. This is how the desire arises to become free of all need, what we call pride.

God doesn't hide himself from them. Sometimes they close their eyes and their hearts to him. Sometimes, they look in the wrong places.

And honestly, so do I. Every day, I commit little acts of pride that close the door on mercy and leave me alone in a room being god of my own little domain. Pride is a tricky thing. It can look like trying hard to please, and then trying even harder. It can look like wanting to win approval, or wanting to control one's surroundings to such a degree that all appears perfect while inside there roils sheer terror at the perceptibility of flaws.

Life in a fallen world has taught us to hide behind masks. Over time, we move from the simple, trusting faith of a child to the insincerity that comes with the wear of the world.

But we can beg for his mercy—for the ability to turn it all over to God, and so be filled with his power to accomplish what he desires for our lives! And there we will find true peace and true freedom.

God wants us to know him. Further, he wants us to know that we need him. We can't make someone holy. We can't even make ourselves holy. When we cooperate with his grace, God does that for us. What we can do is pray for holiness for ourselves and for the people we love. We can pray that our dear Lord will grant us all the merciful grace we need to have both the wisdom that comes from walking closely with him, and an utter childlike dependency on him, even as we age.

Elizabeth Foss

The flourishing of a Christian community depends on the willingness of each of its members to fully accept God's mercy and then to be molded into a new creation. It's not always easy to accept mercy. It requires vulnerability and humility. How do you open yourself to mercy? How does being an apostle of mercy aid the Christian community with whom you love and worship God?

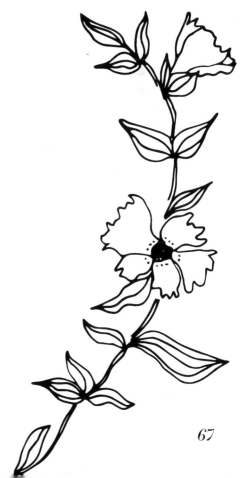

OPEN YOUR BIBLE

ROMANS
CHAPTER 10

SCRIPTURE NOTES:

Focus Verse

But how are they to call on one in whom they have not believed? And how are they to believe in one of whom they have never heard? And how are they to hear without someone to proclaim him? And how are they to proclaim him unless they are sent? As it is written, "How beautiful are the feet of those who bring good news!" But not all have obeyed the good news; for Isaiah says, "Lord, who has believed our message?" So faith comes from what is heard, and what is heard comes through the word of Christ.

Romans 10:14-17

CONSIDER THE COMPONENTS OF LECTIO DIVINA

read	*meditate*
pray	*contemplate*

Day Seventeen

For the first fourteen years of my life, I was ensconced in a fully Catholic community. My parents were (and are) practicing Catholics, as were all my grandparents, aunts, uncles, and cousins. I attended Catholic school, so all my friends were Catholic. Sure, there were a few non-Catholics here and there; one of my classmates was Baptist, and another was a Buddhist, but that was the extent of my contact with non-Catholics.

It wasn't until I was fourteen and began attending the local public high school that I ran into other Christians—and it was perplexing.

"Are you saved?" a classmate asked me at lunch one day.

After swallowing a bite of my sandwich, I nodded. "I'm Catholic," I said this like it was obvious.

My tablemates exchanged looks.

"Oh," my questioner said. "Well, no, you're not saved. You're Catholic."

I looked at them, confused. What on earth were they talking about? We hadn't covered this in religion class. I was Catholic, of course I was saved—weren't all Christians?

I encountered more of this throughout my time in high school. My town is about 90% Evangelical Lutheran, and, for many of my classmates, I was the first Catholic they'd ever met. I was a strange specimen to them. They began to ask me questions that I couldn't answer.

Instead of turning away from my faith, I dove into it. I pulled out the new-at-the-time *Catechism of the Catholic Church* and began to read about the Eucharist, about faith and works, about the papacy. As I read, I knew I wasn't just "confess[ing] with [my] lips" (Romans 14:10)—now I knew why I believed what I believed. These beliefs made logical sense, and I assented to them. The seeds that had been planted in fertile soil and watered for many years were now bearing fruit. (Matthew 13:1-23)

From then on, I knew I could answer people's questions both confidently and respectfully. In the book *I Believe In Love*, Fr. Jean C. J. D'Elbée makes a good point about this:

> For it is not always easy to defend truth and justice—and they need defending—while preserving respect and love of neighbor. Pray with gentleness and humility; calm the passions; ask for light. You will be judged by God of the purity of your intentions.

Gentleness and humility were especially important when I was asked questions in the workplace, where it was known that I was not just Catholic, but a "real Catholic," as one of them said. I became a somewhat reluctant preacher as I answered theological questions at lunch, when what I really wanted to do was eat my taco salad in peace.

Sometimes I dislike being the token Catholic. I dislike being the one who stands out, the one who goes to a different church and has a crucifix on her living room wall, rosaries on the end tables, and theology books on the kitchen table. But at the same time, I know that this is part of my vocation. I have to preach that good news, whenever I'm called to do it, even if it's inconvenient for me (2 Timothy 4:2). If I really love Jesus, and believe in him in my heart, then I can't help but preach.

In order to be an effective preacher, I have to be a person of prayer. I have to spend time with Jesus in order to take him to the people I encounter. I have to study, so I can explain what I believe, and I have to frequent the sacraments, to give me the strength I need to be a missionary, no matter how reluctant. I cannot spread the good news without intimate contact with Jesus, who is the source of the good news.

Emily DeArdo

In this section of Romans, Paul reminds us that it is our faith that saves us—and that faith is accessible to everyone. But one of our jobs as Christians is to bear the good news to others, in order to make salvation known and accessible to all. When our faith flourishes, our response is to offer the overflow to our neighbor. Who has been a bearer of the good news to you? Where are your beautiful feet bringing the good news in your life? Why do you feel compelled to share Christ with others?

OPEN YOUR BIBLE

ROMANS
11:1-15

SCRIPTURE NOTES:

Focus Verse

Now I am speaking to you Gentiles. Inasmuch then as I am an apostle to the Gentiles, I glorify my ministry in order to make my own people jealous, and thus save some of them. For if their rejection is the reconciliation of the world, what will their acceptance be but life from the dead!

Romans 11:13-15

CONSIDER THE COMPONENTS OF LECTIO DIVINA

read	*meditate*
pray	*contemplate*

Day Eighteen

One of my favorite praise songs has a seemingly endless chorus about how God loves us. It's a beautiful, comforting reminder. But its striking first line has always given me pause as it proclaims God to be jealous.

To speak of jealousy in a context of holiness is jarring. We have been conditioned to avoid the desire for what someone else has at all costs. But "jealous," while it usually has a negative connotation, is also defined in the Merriam-Webster Dictionary as "vigilant in guarding a possession."

In this section of his letter to the church community in Rome, Paul addresses the challenge of rooting the gospel in the hearts of two different sectors of that community, the Jews and the Gentiles. He recognizes that the fact that the gospel was "meant for" the Jewish people gives them a sense of some ownership of it, even though they may not have fully accepted it. Thus the newly fervent faith of the Gentiles can be a cause of tension in the young church in Rome.

But Paul also recognizes that, while unwillingness to accept the gospel when it was first preached was not God's plan for his chosen people, the Israelites, a unique opportunity arises from their witness of the Gentiles' fervent faith. This salvation in Christ that is being accepted far and wide is theirs. It was meant for them. If the faith of the Gentiles elicits a jealous desire to protect what is their own and finally moves their hearts to conversion, then a great purpose has been fulfilled, and the church of Rome produces a harvest of first fruits worth celebrating with joy.

Jealousy for the gospel is, at the end of the day, jealousy for the love of God. When we see the faith that someone else has and experience a natural desire to want it for our own, a great purpose has been fulfilled. Our own hearts crave the love of a God who also loves us with a jealous love—a love that calls us his own and vigilantly guards us for himself when we accept that love. We flourish in our faith when we allow the weight of God's mighty love for us to bend our hearts toward him and give our hearts to him singularly. And the message of the gospel flourishes when our faith in God's love and mercy is witnessed by others who then desire what we have.

I remember a rare, serendipitous moment I had, spending a couple of hours on a drive alone with my nephew, a young man in his early twenties who was still trying to work out what life might look like for him as an adult. As we talked, I never intended to try to evangelize him or preach the gospel to him in any direct fashion. I was simply sharing about where I was in my own life and taking the time to get to know more about where he was and how he was doing. But there is little in my own life that does not in some way reflect my faith and my experience of Christ's love and mercy. Unintentionally, as I shared my own story, I was weaving a tale of love and mercy that piqued a curious desire in my nephew's heart. He suddenly turned to me and said, "You see, Nanny Colleen, I want to live my life with that kind of passion and purpose. That kind of certainty and joy."

I stopped and thought about that. There are few things in my life I could say I am certain of. And I am not completely sure what my purpose is in any given moment. But I do know this for sure—that I am loved and treasured by a God who made me, gave his life that I might live, and desires my love.

And that is all this young man needed to see to experience that same twinge of jealousy Paul was eager to see in the Jewish community in Rome. A jealousy that wants to claim that holy love as its own, and return the love of a jealous God who wants to lay claim to our hearts as his own possession.

Colleen Connell

The jealous love of God, which is a heart that does not want to share you with any other god or idol or sin, is a provocative thought for us. It is echoed here in Romans in Paul's heart for the conversion of both the Jews and the Gentiles. It may seem strange to hear his reasoning for making the Israelites jealous in order for them to be saved, but the truth is that God's jealous love wants us to love him with that same kind of hunger and zeal that he has for us. What does it look like to live with a fire for your salvation burning in you? What have you seen in the flourishing of your Christian community that stokes that fire?

OPEN YOUR BIBLE

ROMANS

11:16-36

SCRIPTURE NOTES:

Focus Verse

Just as you were once disobedient to
God but have now received mercy
because of their disobedience, so they
have now been disobedient in order
that, by the mercy shown to you, they
too may now receive mercy. For God
has imprisoned all in disobedience so
that he may be merciful to all.
Romans 11:30-32

CONSIDER THE COMPONENTS OF LECTIO DIVINA

read	*meditate*
pray	*contemplate*

Day Nineteen

At times, the days leading up to Sunday Mass are long and filled with one failure after another—failures that might include hurting someone I love with words of malice or the silence of indifference, or maybe failing in my tasks as wife and mother. It's possible that I've even spread gossip or slandered someone's good name. By the time I get to Saturday, I want a do-over, a clean start. I'm desperate to go to confession so God's mercy can heal my heavy heart.

It never fails to amaze me that before I go in to speak with the priest, my legs feel heavy, I keep my eyes downcast, and the shame makes me feel physically ill. Then, after I receive absolution from our Lord God, I'm filled with love and gratitude, so grateful to God for his infinite mercy and unlimited forgiveness.

This life-changing ritual of monthly confession began in college with a particularly intense confession moment. When I hesitated while confessing my sins, the priest asked me a simple question.

"Mary, do you believe that God truly forgives you for your wrongdoing?"

I was dumbfounded. How did he know my deepest fear? How did he know I'd been questioning God's mercy? How did he know I didn't feel worthy of God's love or forgiveness?

I whispered, "Not always."

It was an honest answer, raw with emotion. I'd been holding on to some sins, clinging to their familiarity and comfort. I was so sure that God couldn't forgive them. My heart raced and my hands were sweaty. I thought the priest was going to take away my Catholic card at any moment and throw me out of the confessional.

Instead he met me with a gentle grace that changed the course of my life.

"Oh, Mary. God loves you with reckless abandon. There is nothing you have to do to earn that love. It's just there. Always there. He forgives your sin with oceans and oceans of mercy. Why are you still hiding your sin from him? What has made you so afraid of God? Give it all over to him so he can heal and restore. He cannot forgive what you will not give him freely and fully. He is waiting right now to love you, no matter what you have done."

I had heard this my whole life, but I didn't really believe it until that afternoon. The priest's kind eyes and easy smile made me feel at ease. I took a deep breath and stepped out in faith. In that moment, the dam broke and my heart burst. I wept as I confessed sins I had held in my heart for years. I gave God everything.

Today's reading talks about God's mercy. He knows we are going to fall and he offers himself as the solution to all pain and suffering. He is the vine of life and we can be grafted on at any time. All we have to do is humble ourselves and ask for his mercy.

A few Sundays ago, I found myself at Mass singing "There's a Wideness in God's Mercy," written by Fr. Frederick Faber, a Catholic priest, in the 1860s. I was struck immediately by the song's lyrics:

There's a wideness in God's mercy
like the wideness of the sea;
there's a kindness in God's justice,
which is more than liberty.

As I sang, I remembered what Paul says in today's reading from Romans: "Just as you were once disobedient to God but now received mercy...For God has imprisoned all in disobedience so that he may be merciful to all." (Romans 11:30, 32)

In spite of my sin and turning away from him in shame, God pursues me every day. He leaves the ninety-nine sheep to find me tangled in the thicket. He tears down any wall I put up because of fear or feeling unworthy of his love. He is relentless in his pursuit of me—and the same goes for you, my dear sister.

Turn to him and allow his mercy and forgiveness to change your heart and heal your life. Our God loves beyond comprehension. It is never too late to begin again.

Mary Lenaburg

All of us are enemies of the gospel at times, wild branches worthy of being cut off from the vine of God's love. But instead, he grants us mercy, which is as equally accessible to all as it is needed by all. What gives you faith in God's mercy for yourself and for others? When have you been awed by the generous gift of his mercy?

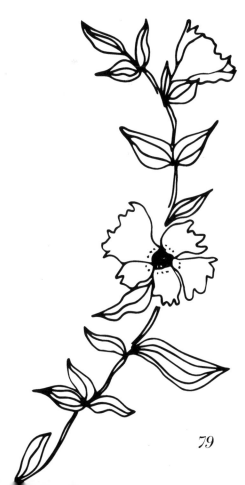

OPEN YOUR BIBLE

ROMANS
CHAPTER 12

SCRIPTURE NOTES:

Focus Verse

I appeal to you therefore, brothers and sisters, by the mercies of God, to present your bodies as a living sacrifice, holy and acceptable to God, which is your spiritual worship. Do not be conformed to this world, but be transformed by the renewing of your minds, so that you may discern what is the will of God—what is good and acceptable and perfect.

Romans 12:1-2

FOR FURTHER READING:

Ephesians 4
Colossians 3:1-17

CONSIDER THE COMPONENTS OF LECTIO DIVINA

read	*meditate*
pray	*contemplate*

Day Twenty

It may have something to do with having spent the summer after second grade obsessed with *All My Children*, but I've always been fascinated by amnesia. Why was it, I wondered, that people forgot their names but not their first language? Why did they struggle to find their way around their homes but have no trouble remembering how to use a spoon or wash their hands?

It's a mercy, I suppose, that those types of memory are different. Imagine if you had to relearn how to brush your teeth, get dressed, read, and drive while also trying to figure out who you are and who everyone else is. Could there be anything more overwhelming?

I think this chapter of Romans can read like just such a herculean task. Paul invites us to offer our bodies as living sacrifices, offering our struggles as a gift to the Lord as we attempt to be transformed by the gospel. We stand up straighter as we vow never to conform ourselves to this world, "to clothe yourselves with the new self, created according to the likeness of God in true righteousness and holiness," as Paul says in Ephesians 4:24.

But then he starts to elaborate. And his description of the Christian life goes on. And on. In this chapter and in the ones that follow. And in other Epistles. And from later saints and councils and popes, in catechisms both local and universal, until it seems that the Christian life is just a matter of rules—thousands upon thousands of rules. Around every corner is a different way you can mess up, and you're no better off than an amnesiac trying to navigate an unfamiliar life.

In a sense, that's exactly what you are. The "thousands" of rules aren't arbitrary restrictions imposed from without in an attempt to snare us and send us to hell, they're a reminder of how we were made. We've forgotten who we are as new men and women in Christ, and the Church is trying to remind us.

Why should we avoid sin? Not merely to keep from being damned, nor even just to please God, but because that's not who we are. "For you have died," Paul says, "and your life is hidden with Christ in God." (Colossians 3:3) You are no longer the woman you used to be. In Christ, you have been made new. So love, serve, rejoice, bless, and forgive—not so that you can earn God's love but because you are a new creation in Christ.

There's no room for complacency but neither is there room for discouragement. And it's easy to get discouraged; after all, we may have been reborn in baptism and again with each confession, but we're still walking in the patterns of the old man we supposedly put to death. So each time we fall, we berate ourselves.

What if instead we reminded ourselves gently, as we would an amnesiac, "This is not who you are." When I find myself gossiping: "No, Meg, this is not who you are." When anger threatens to overcome me: "This is not who you are." When pride drives my every move: "Stop. You are Christ's. This? This is not who you are."

The call to holiness isn't a question of conforming ourselves to arbitrary regulations, but of being reminded again and again of who we are. "No, you use your knife with this hand. This is the chair you like to sit in. These are the books you read. This is your best friend. This is your dog. Stand on the right side of the escalator. Red means stop." Those rules imposed on an amnesiac bring freedom, because they make him the man he truly is.

May these words from St. Paul help us to become who we are.

Meg Hunter-Kilmer

The gift of mercy that is ours spurs an outpouring of love within us. It becomes imperative to live and love well and to put our faith into action, and to let that love unite us to one another. How does the gospel message spill over as love in your life? In what ways does it unite you to others?

Savor

Almond Biscotti

INGREDIENTS

4 whole eggs

2 egg yolks

1 c sugar

1 tsp almond extract

3/4 c roasted almonds

1/2 c melted butter

3 1/2 c flour (divided to 2c and 1 1/2c)

4 tbsp baking powder

DIRECTIONS

Preheat oven to 325 degrees Fahrenheit.

Beat whole eggs and egg yolks in a mixing bowl, adding in the sugar and almond extract.

Add in 1 1/2 c flour into the egg mixture bowl and mix well. Fold in almonds and add melted butter, then the last 2 c of flour.

Form dough into 4 long loaves or 2 larger loaves if you want longer cookies.

Bake loaves for 35 minutes or until light brown and firm.

Remove loaves and let stand for a few minutes to cool for slicing.

Slice 1 inch cookies, placing each back on the pan face up.

Finish baking at 325 degrees Fahrenheit to a golden brown.

Allow to cool and serve.

Dip in melted chocolate for extra decadence.

flourish

a day for Selah

Use this day for pause, prayer, praise, and rest.

Day Twenty-two

Memory

V E R S E

Week Four

**May the God of hope fill you with
all joy and peace in believing, so
that you may abound in hope by the
power of the Holy Spirit.**

ROMANS 15:13

I will practice Scripture memory by:

○ Praying

○ Writing

○ Speaking

○ Reading

○ Other: _____

May the God of hope fill you with all joy and peace in believing

ROMANS 15:13

OPEN YOUR BIBLE

ROMANS
CHAPTER 13

SCRIPTURE NOTES:

Focus Verse

Owe no one anything, except to love
one another; for the one who loves
another has fulfilled the law.

Romans 13:8

CONSIDER THE COMPONENTS OF LECTIO DIVINA

read	*meditate*
pray	*contemplate*

Day Twenty-three

I'm a rule follower. I'm the girl who loads six kids into the car after grocery shopping and, when she finds the pack of gum the checker overlooked, puts everyone back in the cart and goes in to give the store her seventy-nine cents. Because, rules.

I love rules. I love the structure they give to my life, and if I'm honest, I love authority. It's good to know someone else is in charge. But what does St. Paul tell us about defying authority (or not)? It turns out that even though the Roman government was persecuting early Christians, Paul wasn't anti-government or even anti-Roman. He was all about working from within.

The Bible is replete with heroic stories of rule-breakers. Moses defied the pharaoh, leading the Israelites out of Egypt. And God took care of him. Daniel and his friends Shadrach, Mesach, and Abednego all defied their king and refused to worship idols, even though such worship was the law of the land. And God took care of them, too.

Defying authority for Christ doesn't always end well from a mortal perspective. St. Stephen was brave in the face of authority, and he was stoned to death for witnessing to Christ's authority. St. Paul himself was put in jail and ultimately martyred by the Roman authorities for defying the government to proclaim the gospel.

So which is it? Obey the state or not? God saves the follower who is defiant for the Kingdom or not?

We are citizens of heaven first, and we owe our first obedience, always, to the God of heaven and earth. But St. Paul sees the need for us to have a foundation for living a Christian life here in the earthly realm. Because, we do live here, yes?

Note he's not addressing what a Christian should do against an evil regime. Instead, he begins by telling Christians to be obedient to the government because God appointed the authority (Romans 13:1). St. John Chrysostom affirms that the Roman government was "the work of God's wisdom." It's not a perfect government, and there is no question Christians were persecuted.

St. Paul has two tasks at hand. First, he wants to help the Christian community simultaneously understand how to be good citizens and faithful followers of Christ. Then, he also endeavors to persuade the Roman authorities that Christians aren't a threat to be destroyed. When advising Christian obedience, he seizes an opportunity to evangelize the authorities and to persuade them not to punish disciples of Christ.

We cannot ever lose sight of the fact that St. Paul instructs early Christians to honor the government, while also assuming that they will do so within the context of the entire story of salvation history, never forgetting the foundational fact that Jesus Christ is lord of the universe. He knew that those early Christians knew the stories of biblical heroes who died being obedient to God's primary rules for living. Faithful Christians can always wholeheartedly obey the laws of the land as long as those laws don't contradict any of God's laws.

First and foremost, the early Christians—and we—are obedient unto Christ. When we are mindfully obedient to civil authorities, it is always and only because we have given our allegiance to God, who demands that we obey all just laws. Simply, we have one lord and master, and all obedience is ordered to him. We obey the government because of Christ, not despite Christ. Our behavior as a citizen of the state finds its genesis in our identity as a citizen of the city of God.

Ultimately, we live under the rule of love. Love is the fulfillment of the law. St. Paul reminds us to be vigilant, to wake up and recognize that Christ has saved us and that he will come again. We have to live our lives in a way that fulfills the law of love without exception. This is an Advent message: Christ came as a babe in the manger; he descends into souls by grace; and he will come again to judge the living and the dead.

May we be prepared as we live as peaceful citizens of earthly communities to be welcomed into the fullness of the kingdom of the heaven.

Elizabeth Foss

To live as Christians in the world, we honor and respect the systems put in place to govern our community, but we lead and live by the law of love. We live wide awake to the reality of the eternity that awaits us, and we do everything by the light of that reality. What does it look like to for you to "put on the armor of light" (Romans 13:2) and fulfill the law of love? What flourishing comes from that endeavor?

OPEN YOUR BIBLE

ROMANS
CHAPTER 4

SCRIPTURE NOTES:

Focus Verse

For the kingdom of God is not food and
drink but righteousness and peace and
joy in the Holy Spirit. The one who thus
serves Christ is acceptable to God and
has human approval. Let us then pursue
what makes for peace and for mutual
upbuilding.

Romans 14:17-19

CONSIDER THE COMPONENTS OF LECTIO DIVINA

read		*meditate*	
pray		*contemplate*	

Day Twenty-four

I am blessed to have many wonderful friends. These are friends of many years, even decades, that I have shared life with, from the daily to the extraordinary, in good and bad times. I love doing life with them, and they are precious to me.

Most of these women are not Catholic.

To some people, this would be a huge stumbling block. How can you be true friends with people who disagree with you on something so fundamental? This is beyond what Paul talks about in today's reading isn't it? This is about the very nature of God.

There are many differences between Catholics and Protestants, and I'm not going to sugarcoat that. But if we say that we can only be friends with people who think like us, worship like us, and live like us, then we're going to miss out on so many wonderful things that God wants to give us! Let me give you a few examples.

My friend Sarah taught me to knit. We love to talk about books and and our shared love of tea and music and travel. She lives in North Carolina and is married to a high school friend of mine, and even though we're far apart physically, we try to make time to talk at least once a month, by having "virtual tea" with each other using Facebook Messenger or texts. When I was undergoing a huge life change and faith challenge, Sarah was there with prayers, support, and care packages. I delight in her children, Lydia and Paul Michael, and in her heart for ministry. Sarah also has a master's degree in divinity, and she's been a pastor at several churches. You would think that we'd be diametrically opposed to one another because of our beliefs. But when we talk about faith, we do it in a respectful way, in an open dialogue focused on learning about the other's belief, not changing them. We delight in sharing our hearts and lives with each other. We don't believe exactly the same things, but we have "righteousness and peace and joy in the Holy Spirit." (Romans 14:17)

My best friend Tiffany and I have known each other since we were fourteen and were seated next to each other in drama class. She is an evangelical Lutheran. But that doesn't stop us from having spent more than twenty years as best friends. I've gone on vacation with her family, rejoiced in her marriage to a wonderful man, and spent many summer evenings binge-watching movies at her house. She's visited me during my numerous hospitalizations, and she's the reason I discovered my deep love for Jane Austen when she lent me the six-hour *Pride and Prejudice* miniseries. She has qualities such as patience, flexibility, and unerring good humor that I wish I had myself.

Both Sarah and Tiffany understand me and love me just as I am, which is no small feat. To have someone who sees you and knows you and loves you, just as you are? That's a true gift from God.

God orchestrates our lives perfectly, bringing people in and out like a skilled conductor brings in sections of an orchestra according to the score. We can't see his divine plan, so we need to trust him. The people in your life are not there by accident. They are there for "mutual upbuilding" (Romans 14:20); they're there to enrich your life. Meet these people, and "walk in love, as Christ loved us and gave himself up for us, a fragrant offering and sacrifice to God" (Ephesians 5:2) as long as they are in your life. If a friendship is rooted in God, it will bear good and lasting fruit.

Emily DeArdo

Forming a Christian community of people of Jewish backgrounds and pagan backgrounds could not have been easy for the young Roman church. Surely there were different ideas of worship and living the Christian life that could have put the community at odds. After his treatise on living the law of love in Romans 14, Paul focuses on not letting judgment cause destruction to the good God has called us to do for and with one another as a Christian community. How have you overcome differences and set aside judgment in order to see goodness flourish in your life?

OPEN YOUR BIBLE

ROMANS
15:1-13

SCRIPTURE NOTES:

Focus Verse

May the God of steadfastness and
encouragement grant you to live in
harmony with one another, in accordance
with Christ Jesus, so that together you may
with one voice glorify the God and Father
of our Lord Jesus Christ.

Romans 15:5-6

CONSIDER THE COMPONENTS OF LECTIO DIVINA

read	*meditate*
pray	*contemplate*

Day Twenty-five

Every Sunday in college, after a hearty brunch, we would gather around the piano. One person would settle on the bench to lead and play the choir parts. Each voice joined in, taking a part according to his or her ability. The dozen or so of us had just been together doing much of the same only an hour before. Congregating in the early hours of the morning, we'd rise long before most of the campus' residents, who were using the weekend hours attempting to catch up on their sleep. We'd practice an hour before Mass, sing throughout the two hour liturgy, and return to lifting our voices once again after filling our rumbling stomachs, this time without an agenda. It seemed we could never get our fill of raising our voices together in song.

The harmonious melodies that resulted in the music we created together felt like a touching of the heavens. It was a manifestation of the hidden cosmos. Much of what we sang was in praise of the Lord, but even when it wasn't directly, it still did just that as we created what was invisible with our voices.

There was a certain "deficiency" as individuals, as we were unable to produce alone the layered polyphony that became present as we harmonized. Our separate voices were beautiful of their own accord but together they produced a harmony that was difficult to describe. It settled the mind. It brought peace to the soul. The sound could raise the hair on your arms and bring tears of joy to your eyes. It was stirring whether one was a participant or merely a witness.

Even before the advent of Christ, Pythagoras taught that the harmony produced in music was revelatory of a greater harmony that exists in the universe, what he called "the music of the spheres." By making music, man participates in the harmony of the universe. He makes it manifest.

When we came together with our voices, we were working together to imitate God's creation. In a way, we were making visible what is invisible to the eye. The unity of our voices became an expression of the stunning harmony veiled within creation.

> May the God of steadfastness and encouragement grant you to
> live in harmony with one another, in accordance with Jesus Christ,
> so that you may with one voice glorify the God and Father of our
> Lord Jesus Christ. (Romans 15:5)

We are all called to move together within this world externalizing the beautiful harmony and unity that, ultimately, is God. Whether through music or some other creative endeavor, whether through worship or some other means of fellowship, whether in our daily endeavors or fantastic feats, we glorify God when we move together in harmony. The community flourishes when all are moving animated by his grace.

Just as in choral singing, when one is floundering, we look for ways to encourage and bring one another up. When one voice is singing off key or the wrong note, it affects the whole choir. Correspondingly, a broken limb in the Body of Christ disrupts the proper functioning of the whole in giving glory to God as we live and move.

We are in this together. No man or woman is better than the other but an integral part of the whole. Let us work out our own salvation with fear and trembling (Philippians 2:12), yes, but always seeking to bring our neighbor alongside us in the process.

For where there is unity, there is God.

Laurel Muff

Paul continues to instruct the Roman church on what it means to create a flourishing Christian community. Here, he enjoins them to live in a spirit of welcome, to pursue peace and harmony, and to cultivate joy. How have you experienced welcome in Christian community? What about worshipping God with others fills you with joy and hope?

OPEN YOUR BIBLE

ROMANS

15:14-33

SCRIPTURE NOTES:

Focus Verse

I myself feel confident about you, my
brothers and sisters, that you yourselves are
full of goodness, filled with all knowledge,
and able to instruct one another.

Romans 15:14

FOR FURTHER READING:
2 Samuel 7:10-17
Habakkuk 2:4

CONSIDER THE COMPONENTS OF LECTIO DIVINA

read	*meditate*
pray	*contemplate*

Day Twenty-six

Picture it—the United States, 2018. The Catholic Church is rocked by the revelation of abuse scandals and cover-ups of the past yet again. There is anger toward the leadership of our institutional Church and continued distrust in the hierarchy. Where were the men sent to lead, to protect the vulnerable? How do we wait for our the clergy to restore the Church?

We don't.

We embrace the reality that this is our Church—that we are the Church. With faithful clergy in our midst, the laity can resolve to ensure that the Church will flourish. We don't have to wait for someone to visit. Even St. Paul, as we read here, could not assure that he would arrive in a timely manner. He is not the solution to the issues the Roman church faces.

Jesus is.

St. Paul begins in this passage by lifting up the church of Rome, saying, "I myself feel confident about you, my brothers and sisters, that you yourselves are full of goodness, filled with all knowledge, and able to instruct one another." (Romans 15:14)

The mystical body is made up of all the baptized and saints—the holy people of God, not a structure.

If anything can be gained by the turmoil that has broken loose yet again, it is that we need to return to our roots. In other words, we must return to the worship of Christ alone—not positions of power, not the protection of structures and a squeaky clean image. We must fix our eyes on unflagging devotion to the gospel—the good news that is still Jesus Christ.

For the body of Christ to flourish, it is up to you and me, dear friends. You and I must embrace the gifts we were given at our baptism. We must fan the flames of the Holy Spirit that were stirred up at our confirmation. We have been given an immense power through the blood of Christ and the anointing of the Spirit. We can no longer abdicate our responsibility to those whose "job" it is. "The holy people of God share also in Christ's prophetic office." (*Lumen Gentium*, 12) A life in Christ, the life of a disciple, is a mission of love—a love of sharing the grace and mercy of Christ and a love of neighbor. It is a lifelong mission, not a one-time project. It is the very thing for which we have been equipped by Christ.

It is up to us to recognize the call on our hearts and the unique way we have been prepared to fulfill it. St. Paul writes to the Corinthians:

> Now there are varieties of gifts, but the same Spirit; and there are varieties of services, but the same Lord; and there are varieties of activities, but it is the same God who activates all of them in everyone. To each is given the manifestation of the Spirit for the common good. (1 Cor. 12:4-7)

We all have a different, but equally important, role to play in building the body of Christ.

Many years ago, when I was first entering ministry, a dear friend introduced me to a work on charisms. Charisms are special abilities given to all Christians by the Holy Spirit to give them power both to represent Christ and to be a channel of God's goodness for people. (cf. CCC 2003) The perspective changed my life. It taught me to cooperate with the grace Jesus pours into me to do his work. If you haven't heard of charisms (and the fact that you have one!), I encourage you to read up. It is a much needed reminder that "the testimony of Christ has been strengthened among you—so that you are not lacking in any spiritual gift as you wait for the revealing of our Lord Jesus Christ." (cf 1 Cor. 1:6-7) In Jesus Christ, we have everything we need. We are empowered by the Spirit to be the voice crying out in the wilderness of our time.

I will leave you with these words of wisdom from Servant of God Catherine Doherty:

> Remember, the Church is the laity as well as the priests and bishops. The laity is also called to be apostles. The great tragedy of our times has its roots in the fact that, for a while, this wondrous and immense truth was forgotten. Under the duress and stress of the Reformation the laity was relegated to a secondary place and lost the vision of its apostolic vocation. It lost the knowledge that ordinary men and women were, in their fashion, a great part of the royal priesthood of Christ.

Rakhi McCormick

Even Paul longed to contribute to and be part of flourishing Christian community. He truly loved the people he served, the people he served alongside, and allowed people to serve him out of love. It is a sign of true humility to live that kind of life. How have you seen all aspects of Christian communal life come together to help you flourish in faith?

ROMANS
CHAPTER 16

SCRIPTURE NOTES:

Focus Verse

For while your obedience is known to all,
so that I rejoice over you, I want you to be
wise in what is good and guileless in what
is evil. The God of peace will shortly crush
Satan under your feet. The grace of our
Lord Jesus Christ be with you.
Romans 16:19-20

FOR FURTHER READING:
John 13:16
1 Peter 5:14
Matthew 7:15-20
Acts 8:2

CONSIDER THE COMPONENTS OF LECTIO DIVINA

read	*meditate*
pray	*contemplate*

Day Twenty-seven

Do you open your Bible expectantly and obediently and then skip the long lists of genealogies, hoping to get to the "good part?" I know that I have done so on more than one occasion. I am eager to get to the story, impatient with the tedious details.

But if we believe that the Bible is the inerrant word of God (and we do), then we have to pause at the lists of names and wonder what message there is for us there. Paul has just written his longest letter; he has given to us the essential gospel, and concludes it with a guest list?

Paul is greeting his friends in Rome and sending greetings from some who were with him in Corinth. He includes these greetings here at the prompting of the Holy Spirit. Here, within this list of St. Paul's friends, we have a snapshot of the church, a picture that shows us that the church is made up of diverse people—ordinary in their own communities—who know Jesus personally, and serve him in their homes and neighborhoods in the daily living with and loving of one another. This chapter is replete with the personal relationships St. Paul had with the people of the early Church, and it reflects his love for the saints who lived and worked with him. Here is our peek into the personal relationships that the theologian Paul had with his Christian friends.

Most of the people in this chapter have Gentile names and most were probably slaves or recently freed men. Some of them are women. At least one, Erastus, was an important public official. Some were single. Prisca and Aquila, who were fellow Jews with Paul, served together as a married couple. And then, there's Rufus, whose father was Simon of Cyrene, the man forced to literally carry Jesus' cross. Together, these are the people who took up that cross after the resurrection and carried it when the Church was new. These are the people Paul offers as examples of believers who are in Christ (Romans 8:1), and these are saints who will not be separated from the love of God (Romans 8:39). Rich and poor, Gentile and Jew, male and female—they belong to God and they live out their lives for his glory. St. Paul has offered to them and to their communities a gospel of sound doctrine, and he warns them not to squander it.

As I work my way through the first fifteen chapters of the letter to the Romans, I can devise a personal rule of life for myself, confident that all the guidelines for holy living are here. But when I read the warm greeting and the personal connections Paul makes to such a long list of people, and I see that he urges them to extend hospitality to one another, I cannot deny that community is essential to the Christian life. This life in Christ is not a solitary endeavor. We are called to live the gospel in relationship with one another. St. Paul knows that relationships can be tricky, and he knows what it is to be hurt by others. He refers to three specific occasions of pain in his second letter to Timothy (2 Tim. 1:15; 4:10, 14). Still, he is insistent on community.

Saints serve. Over and over again, St. Paul reminds the Romans that his friends in Christ are friends in service. We are called to be like Mary whom he says "has worked hard for you" (16:6), called to be diligent "workers in the Lord" (16:12). There is much labor to be done and we are no doubt called to do it. We recall that in chapter twelve, he has told us that each of us has been given spiritual gifts to use to serve so that God may be given the glory. The work will be hard and we will do it together, all the gifts together serving the one Church.

As you reach the end of this magnificent letter, but before you reach the doxology, ponder and pause over each name and the loving description the apostle has for each of his friends. Then, stop to wonder how he would describe you if he were writing today. How do you fit into the picture of the Church? How do you serve?

Finally, move to the blessing and praise. Let each word take root. Then, with prayer, go in peace, glorifying God with your life.

Elizabeth Foss

Remember that Paul had not yet visited the community in Rome when he wrote this letter to them. Yet it seems they had received many visitors and disciples who had come on a mission to strengthen their faith. And just as those disciples had surely come to know the members of the Roman church, each of them is known and loved by Paul. Life in Christ is meant to be lived in communities where we are known, and known by, our brothers and sisters in Christ. What are some steps you have taken or feel called to take to make that happen in your own faith life?

Savor

Homemade Sparkling Lime Seltzer

INGREDIENTS

2-3 limes

1 c sugar

1 c water

seltzer water

DIRECTIONS

Peel back half of the skin of one lime. Cut remaining limes into wedges for garnish.

Create a zesty simple syrup by boiling one cup of water in a small saucepan.

Remove from heat and add sugar, whisking until dissolved. Pour syrup into a air-tight container and place one wedge of lime into syrup to lock in flavor.

Once cooled, pour seltzer over ice and use one tablespoon of syrup per 8 oz of seltzer. Mix with a spoon.

Add lime for garnish.

Mix it up and add different flavors to syrup by trying rosemary, cilantro, orange peel, or mint.

flourish

a day for Selah

Use this day for pause, prayer, praise, and rest.

For our Romans study, *Flourish*, we wanted to offer a fresh book design to celebrate Paul's message that salvation is offered through the gospel of Jesus Christ. This Scripture study is enhanced through a new, clean layout framed with delicate artwork which make us excited to debut these updates and changes. We hope you enjoy what's new and continue to join in Scripture study with us.

For the cover, we kept a minimal white canvas with stark title letters in cutouts of a photo taken in Rome by one of our writers, Colleen Connell. It's a dramatic portrayal of earthly life. Our experiences are viewed through thin keyholes, how we perceive ourselves and our lives but, on the other side, is the full picture: God's truth and love for us. Sometimes we only see darkness, sometimes we only see light, and sometimes we cannot make sense of what we see. We believe the first step to finding answers to our heart's calling is to open our Bibles, to be with God in his Word.

We made a visual biography of Paul, so you have a reference to apply his history and person not only to the word as text, but to apply it to your daily life as both a fellow sinner and follower of Christ.

The interior is where the Word is held and our work is done. The structure invites Scripture notes, followed by an essay and a clean reflection page.

We kept romantic swash calligraphy, hand-lettered, to remind us that the people make up the Church, with the Word at the core of the mission.

As we grow in Scripture memory, we reach for the sun like a vine, so we gave you a growing illustration of a tomato plant to as you work through this journal. Beginning as a seedling, growing into a young plant, flowering, and then producing the fruit of works is how we live out our faith while keeping Scripture as our guide.

The new recipes are a refreshing addition to this study. We created classic takes on traditional recipes that we think you'll enjoy in your kitchen this season. We hope that you can find connection to community through sharing our meals and remember to make each new effort to live out our faith.

We pray that these details help you dig deep into Romans and remember the beautiful gift of the gospel, and, most importantly, that you are a daughter of Christ, made with a special purpose and so loved by God.

Kristin Foss

Art Director

For our Romans study, *Flourish*, we wanted to offer a fresh book design *to celebrate Paul's message that salvation is offered through the gospel of Jesus Christ.*

Why Lectio Divina?

Together, as a community of faithful women, we endeavor to better understand the heart of the gospel and to live it out in our lives. Each day, we invite our souls to encounter our Lord.

How? How will the tired soul living in the woman in the midst of secular culture and busyness still herself and find her Lord? How will she find hope and new energy in the act of one more thing on her to-do list?

She will pray—more. That's right. She will take more time to pray even though so many things pull on her time. Can we do that together? Can we take up for ourselves the ancient tradition of *Lectio Divina* and let the Word lead us to live in charity? We can and we must. This is the best way to prepare ourselves for each day with peaceful composure and serene grace.

In his 2010 apostolic exhortation *Verbum Domini*, Pope Benedict XVI beautifully instructs the faithful to prayerfully read the Scripture. Following his lead, we will be drawn into a practice that is as old as Scripture itself. We will closely read and ponder Scripture passages carefully chosen for this season.

In the early Christian communities, Scripture was read to nourish faith with the wisdom of truth. When we hold the New Testament, we take up the understanding that the first Christians had of the Old Testament, together with the divine revelation the Holy Spirit granted to Jesus' earliest followers.

The Church Fathers' faith was informed by their careful, prayerful reading of the word. Today, we are blessed to welcome their wisdom into our reading when we access the commentaries that were the fruit of their lectio. The monastic movement grew in the fertile soil of *Lectio Divina*. The daily, ordered life of the monks was (and is) centered upon spiritual reading of Scripture. Can ordinary women in the twenty-first century find spiritual nourishment and new life in this age-old practice of holy men?

We can.

There are five steps in the pattern, five distinct movements that will direct the way we travel through our days. First, we read. Then, a meditation engages the mind, using reason to search for knowledge in the message. The prayer is the movement of the heart towards God, a beseeching on behalf of the soul. The contemplation elevates the mind and suspends it in God's presence. Finally, the action is the way we live our lives as a gift of charity towards others. It's a tall order, but it's the very best way to live.

Let's take a careful look at each step.

Pope Benedict writes, "It opens with the reading (*lectio*) of a text, which leads to a desire to understand its true content: what does the biblical text say in itself." (*Verbum Domini*, 87) This is where we explore the literary genre of the text, the characters we meet in the story, and the objective meaning intended by the author. We usually offer several passages which work together towards a common theme; you can choose just one passage, or you can look at the group together, as the Holy Spirit inspires. A good study Bible and/or a Bible dictionary will help you to place the reading in context.

"Next comes meditation (*meditatio*), which asks: what does the biblical text say to us?" (DV, 87) Prayerfully we ponder what personal message the text holds for each of us and what effect that message should have on our lives.

"Following this comes prayer (*oratio*), which asks the question: what do we say to the Lord in response to his word? Prayer, as petition, intercession, thanksgiving and praise, is the primary way by which the word transforms us." (DV, 87). What do we say to God in response to his Word? We ask him what he desires of us. We ask him for the strength and grace to do his will. Moved by his mercy, we give him thanks and praise.

The fourth act is "contemplation (*contemplatio*), during which we take up, as a gift from God, his own way of seeing and judging reality, and ask ourselves what conversion of mind, heart and life is the Lord asking of us?" (DV, 87) Here, reflect on how God has conveyed his love for us in the day's Scripture. Recognize the beauty of his gifts and the goodness of his mercy and rest in that. Let God light you from within and look out on the world in a new way because you have been transformed by the process of prayerful Scripture study.

Finally, the whole point of this time we've taken from our day is to get up from the reading and go live the gospel. Actio is where we make an act of our wills and resolve to bring the text to life in our lives.

This is our fiat.

> The process of *Lectio Divina* is not concluded until it arrives at action (*actio*), which moves the believer to make his or her life a gift for others in charity. We find the supreme synthesis and fulfillment of this process in the Mother of God. For every member of the faithful Mary is the model of docile acceptance of God's word, for she "kept all these things, pondering them in her heart." (Lk 2:19; cf. 2:51) (DV, 87)

As a community at Take Up & Read, we will endeavor to engage in *Lectio Divina* every day. To correlate with each day's Scripture passages, we've created pages for your time of prayer, and we've created pages for your active time. We want this book to come alive in your hands, to bring you a spiritual springtime. Try to take the time each day to dig deep, but if you have to cut your time short, don't be discouraged. Ask the Blessed Mother to help you find pockets throughout the day to re-engage. You don't have to fill in every box. There is no right or wrong answer. And you don't have to dig deeply with every passage.

Pray the parts you can, and trust the Holy Spirit to water it well in your soul. Know that God can do loaves and fishes miracles with your small parcels of time, if only you are willing to offer him what you have. Before your days—and then your weeks—get swallowed with the ordinary to-do lists of life's hustle, sit in prayer and see how you can tune your heart to the beat of the Lord's, and ensure that the best gift you give is your life, poured out for others in charity.

Ask the Blessed Mother to help you find pockets throughout the day to re-engage. You don't have to fill in every box. There is no right or wrong answer. And you don't have to dig deeply with every passage.

Meet the Authors

Micaela Darr is a California girl, born and raised, with brief stints in Mexico, Spain, and South Korea. She's extroverted by nature, but being a mom of seven kids has driven her to appreciate having quiet alone time, too. Her husband Kevin is the best in the world, especially because he's exceedingly patient in regards to her harebrained schemes (see: living in South Korea). Micaela is disorganized by nature, but is also bound and determined to improve herself in that area and has done so with a modicum of success. She loves to read, watch good TV, and chat your ear off.

Emily DeArdo is a central Ohio native who can often be found with tea in one hand and a book in the other (or knitting needles, or her sketchbook). She is the oldest of three children and loves Eucharistic Adoration, re-reading Jane Austen, and cheering for the Pittsburgh Penguins. Along with St. Thomas Aquinas, she believes that hot baths, sleep, and good drinks (in her case, tea or Diet Coke) cure most things. She is also a wickedly competitive Trivial Pursuit player and musical theater nerd.

Elizabeth Foss spends her days (and some nights) seeking beauty and truth and then searching for just the right words to express what she's found. The Founder and Content Director of Take Up & Read, she's astonished and incredibly grateful to have the opportunity to do work she loves with people she loves. Elizabeth lives in Loudoun County, Virginia with her husband and six of her nine kids, but frequently travels south to Charlottesville and north to New York and Connecticut to work (and play) with her grown children.

Katy Greiner thinks all mornings would be better if they started with the Dexys Midnight Runner's classic "Come On, Eileen." Her favorite way to waste time is by consuming quality long-form journalism that provokes Big Thoughts, and therefore good conversation. When she's not looking over her shoulder for the real adult in the room to take care of her high school freshmen, she's planning her next trip or craving Chick-Fil-A. She loves a good sunset, talking over texting, tea over coffee, all kinds of music, and hearing God laugh.

Ana Hahn is a wife of nine years and mother of five. She enjoys educating her three school-aged daughters at home and playing planes with her two toddler boys. In her rare spare time she works on making her home bright and cheerful.

Meg Hunter-Kilmer is a hobo missionary who lives out of her car and travels around the world giving talks and retreats; in her heart, though, she lives in a house surrounded by lilacs in a small town in the South and spends her afternoons on the front porch with a stack of Young Adult princess books and a plate full of pastries. That not being an option, she spends much of her time making small talk, listening to audiobooks, and hunting down unlocked churches where she can make a holy hour. She hates bananas with a burning passion and used to keep a guitar pick in her wallet just in case—despite the fact that she doesn't play guitar.

Mary Lenaburg relishes entertaining. Her door is always open and the coffee hot. When traveling to speak, she love to explore the local candy shops looking for the perfect dark chocolate fudge (with nuts is best). Mary spends her free time reading the latest best selling murder mystery and baking her famous chocolate chip cookies, assuring that the kitchen cookie jar is always full. Mary and her husband have been happily married for thirty years, finding joy among the ashes, having lost their disabled daughter Courtney in 2014. They live in Northern Virginia with their grown son Jonathan.

Rakhi McCormick is a convert from Hinduism who currently resides in the Metro Detroit area, often chasing after her three young children and husband. Rakhi is a terrible housekeeper, but enjoys a beautiful home. She is a lover of all things Italy and St. Teresa of Calcutta, with a quiet demeanor but fiery spirit. You can often find her mid-project, creating pretty things amid the chaos and singing along to Spotify all with a coffee in hand.

Allison McGinley recently moved to the Philly suburbs with her husband and two kids, and is living her dream with a church, library, and diner within walking distance. She returned to her faith during college, and nothing has been the same ever since, in the best way. Writing is the way she processes life and discovers the beauty all around her, and she's been known to write in her closet in the middle of the night when the right words were suddenly found. She's happiest when taking photos of beautiful things, worshipping God through song, drinking a cup of coffee, or standing by the ocean.

Colleen Connell is a bringer-upper-of-boys and wanna-be saint who packs a little Louisiana spice with her wherever she goes. She currently serves at-risk families in her job as a social worker in Fort Wayne, Indiana, and spends copious hours on football and soccer fields yelling more loudly than all the other moms. She finds joy in the Word, the world, and the wild wonder of everyday life

Laurel Muff is a California girl who loves to travel, write, knit, read, and sing (but not necessarily in that order). She is married to her best friend and they have two beautiful girls together, whom she teaches at home. She loves to gather people around the table for delicious food and great conversation. With a heart for ministry, she is glad to share her faith in whatever capacity the Lord beckons her.

Heather Renshaw is a wife and mother of five living in the missionary territory of the Pacific Northwest. She loves deep conversation, loud singing, good eating, and silent Adoration. When she's not tackling the myriad tasks of her domestic church, Heather enjoys speaking at events, connecting on social media, and dreaming big dreams.

Kate Wicker is a wife, mom of five, author, speaker, and a recovering perfectionist. She loves reading, running, shoes, God, and encouraging women to embrace the messiness of life instead of trying to cover it up, make excuses for it, or feeling ashamed of their brokenness or their home's sticky counters. From her home in Athens, Georgia, Kate strives every single, imperfect day to strike a balance between keeping it real and keeping it joyful.

Meet the Artist

Kristin Foss is the Art Director and Designer for Take Up & Read. She is a self-taught artist who focuses on bright hues and details. With a paintbrush in her hand and fresh cut foliage in a vase, she finds peace in God's Word while putting brush to paper. Her studio is located in the countryside of Connecticut where she lives with her four children and husband. She enjoys painting, cooking, thrifting, and gardening.

Consider the Lilies: Maybe this is a difficult season in your life—you're overwhelmed by the burdens weighing you down, the crosses the Lord has asked you to carry. This study is for you. It is full of the consolations of the Holy Spirit; he is encouraging you to lament, to pour out your grief and your fears and your anger. Or maybe you're in a sweet spot. Life is really rather good right now. This study is for you, too. It makes you a better friend to the woman next to you, to the growing child who aches, to the spouse who despairs. And it buries words into your heart so that they are there, waiting, when the rain begins to fall. Because it will fall.

Stories of Grace: Here you will find thirty-one days of Jesus' stories carefully collected for you. Along the way, we've provided meditation essays, journaling prompts, space for your notes and drawings, beautiful calligraphy pages, and prayers to draw you deeper into the parables Jesus told. Do you have eyes to see and ears to hear our Lord's stories of grace?

Ponder: An intimate encounter with the rosary, this lovely volume integrates Bible study, journaling, and thoughtful daily action prompts. You will grow in your appreciation and understanding of the beautiful, traditional rosary devotion, while deepening your love for Jesus in the gospel.

Ponder for Kids: Created especially for children, this book contains Bible stories for every mystery of the rosary. Full of interesting things to do, the journal is bursting with discussion questions, personal prayer prompts, puzzles, and coloring pages. There are also nature study pages to create a botanical rosary.

True Friend: Whether a woman is nineteen or forty-nine, friendship with other women can enrich our lives and can make us weep. How do we find friends who are kind and true? By becoming those friends ourselves. This beautiful book invites you to explore what God has to say about lasting friendships.

Bibliography

The Bible. She Reads Truth Christian Standard Bible. Nashville: Holman Bible
Publishers, 2017.

The Didache Bible: With Commentaries Based on the Catechism of the Catholic
Church. San Francisco: Ignatius Press, 2015.

Chrysostom, St. John. The Homilies on the Epistle of St. Paul to the Romans.
Third edition. Oxford: James Parker and Co and Rivingtons, 1877.

Doherty, Catherine. Dear Sister. Bruce Publishing Company, 1953.

D'Elbée, Fr. Jean C.J. I Believe In Love: A Personal Retreat Based on the Teachings of
St. Thérèse of Lisieux. Manchester: Sophia Institute Press, 2001.

Hahn, Scott, general editor. Catholic Bible Dictionary. New York: Doubleday
Religion, 2009.

Hahn, Scott, editor, and Curtis Mitch, compiler. Ignatius Catholic Study Bible: New
Testament. San Francisco: Ignatius Press, 2010.

Ratzinger, Cardinal Joseph and Seewald, Peter. God and the World: Believing and
Living in Our Time. San Francisco: Ignatius Press, 2002.

Reilly, Robert R. "The Music of the Spheres, or the Metaphysics of Music." Intercollegiate
Review, vol. 37, no. 1, 2001, pp. 12-21. https://home.isi.org/music-spheres-or-
metaphysics-music Accessed July 27, 2018.

COLOPHON

This book was printed by CreateSpace, on 55# paper with an interior black and white.
Typefaces used include Futura PT, Essonnes, and Minion Pro.
The cover is printed in full color with a soft touch matte, full laminate.
Finished size is 7" x 10".

Made in the USA
Columbia, SC
07 October 2018